ALSO BY STEFFI BERNE

The Cookie Jar Cookbook

The Teatime Cookbook

The TEATIME *Cookbook*

Tempting Treats and Charming Collectible Teapots

Steffi Berne

PHOTOGRAPHS BY DAVID PHELPS

VILLARD BOOKS
NEW YORK
1995

Library of Congress Cataloging-in-Publication Data
Berne, Steffi.
The teatime cookbook / by Steffi Berne; photographs by David Phelps.
p.   cm.
Includes index.
ISBN 0-679-42144-0
1. Afternoon teas.   I. Title.
TX736.B47   1994
641.5'3—dc20   94-2125

Book design by Debbie Glasserman
Manufactured in Italy on acid-free paper
98765432
First Edition

To Bob and Lizzie and Alex

Acknowledgments

◆

I would like to thank the many friends, acquaintances, and professionals who contributed to this book: my original editor, Emily Bestler, and the others at Villard Books who worked on this project, Amy Edelman, Leta Evanthes, Debbie Glasserman, Andrew Krauss, Lilly Langotsky, Randee Marullo, and Dan Rembert; Julanne Arnold and Kathie Casey Flannery for sharing their recipes; Sheila Lukins for lending her green plate and her support; Lore Mendelsohn and Chiquita Prestwood for allowing us to photograph their cats; Dora Jonassen, David Phelps, and Cathryn Schwing for their good taste and talents; Doe Coover and Lizzie Berne for their counsel; and Pat Pellegrini for her enthusiasm.

Contents

◆

Introduction

◆

I thought I was a one-book gal. I had a great collection of cookie recipes, an excellent collection of cookie jars, and a word processor—all I needed to turn my hobbies into a book. I had a swell time baking and collecting and writing, and when I completed *The Cookie Jar Cookbook* I realized I wasn't finished. I had more cookie recipes, and what about pound cake recipes (I adore pound cake), and the Lady Cake recipe I use for family birthday cakes, and my delicious corn muffins? As for collectibles, I wasn't short of those either: biscuit tins, majolica, measuring cups, advertising kitchenware; but none was the perfect match for the recipes I wanted to write.

In 1991, when my first book was published, afternoon tea was becoming very popular in New York, where I live. Articles about fund-raising teas, power teas, ladies-who-used-to-lunch at tea, schoolboys being taught to pour tea were appearing regularly in newspapers and periodicals. I was the owner of only one novelty teapot then, an adorable yellow duck given to me by my best friend, Sheila. But *The Teapot Cookbook* seemed a natural, so I set out to borrow a collection of teapots to illustrate my recipes. I pored over newsletters and weeklies devoted to antiques and collectibles and was able to locate several teapot collectors, but none, understandably, willing to commit to sending their treasures to me to photograph alongside my teatime foods. Clearly, there was nothing to do but assemble my own collection.

My other collections have taken shape over years, some over decades, but the realities of publishing forced me to gather all the teapots in less than a year. My husband and I traveled to England and spent two wonderful weeks choosing from the wealth of charming teapots available in antique shops, jumble sales, and flea markets. Back home I advertised, shopped, traded, and created a quick collection. I was "hooked" very early in my pursuit, and actually gathered more than twice as many pots as I was able to use in this book. Now I can slow to the pace I am more comfortable with and browse and buy more leisurely because this collection is nowhere near complete.

The popularity of tea continues to grow, perhaps a sign of the slower-paced nineties, when we are more willing to indulge ourselves with a bit of relaxation and sustenance. It seems to me that the foods traditionally served at this highly civilized meal will always be popular—the sweet and savory flavors, the small portions, and, of course, the bracing beverage. During the course of writing *The Teatime Cookbook,* "taking tea" became a daily ritual for me. I recommend it.

The BASICS

Equipment

◆

Baking parchment is used to line cookie sheets and cake pans and makes removal of the baked goods simple and neat. It is available in rolls and in precut sheets and rounds.

Cake pans are described by either their diameter or the length of two sides or their capacity (filled to the top). It is important to use the size called for or risk overflowing, overbaking, underbaking, or generally unsuccessful baking. Pans with a dark or nonstick surface will create baked goods with darker crusts than pans with a light, shiny surface. Pans with a black surface require an oven temperature 25 degrees lower than what is specified in recipes.

Cookie cutters should have edges sharp enough to cut through dough containing nuts and dried fruits.

Cookie sheets should have only one raised side to allow maximum air circulation around the cookies as they bake and for ease of removing parchment or foil liner. Choose sheets that are at least 2 inches shorter and narrower than the inside dimensions of your oven. A shiny surface is preferable because it will reflect heat, not absorb it.

Electric mixers are essential for most cake baking, a standing mixer being more effective than a hand-held one. Most cookie recipes do not require an electric mixer; a wooden spoon is adequate.

Food processors are excellent for chopping nuts, grating quantities of cheese, and preparing pastry crusts and shortbread dough. In most cases where a recipe calls for the use of a processor I provide instructions for preparation without one.

Graters with very small openings are good for removing the zest of citrus fruits. Avoid grating the bitter white pith.

Measuring cups with the maximum measurement marked below the edge of the cup are for liquid ingredients. Dry ingredients are measured in cups that are meant to be filled to overflowing, then swept cleanly across the top with a knife or other straight edge.

Mercury oven thermometers are the most accurate and are recommended. Oven temperatures vary widely, and to avoid mishaps occurring while baking, it is best not to rely on your oven's thermostat.

Racks, usually wire mesh, are essential for cooling baked goods. They should have "feet" to raise them and allow air to circulate below.

Rolling pins come in straight cylinder shapes (best for rolling out squares and rectangles) and in graduated cylinders (best for rolling out rounds).

Rulers are handy in the kitchen for measuring pans and the thickness of dough, and for cutting neat bars and cake portions.

Sifters are used to aerate flour and other dry ingredients. A fine sieve can be used for the same purpose. Do not wash or wet your flour sifter, just shake out any excess and store it in a plastic bag.

Spatulas made of rubber are used for scraping the sides of bowls and for folding ingredients. Wide metal spatulas are better for removing cookies from baking sheets. Narrow, flexible metal spatulas are good for frosting cakes.

Steamed-pudding molds should have tight-fitting covers and usually have decorative designs. An adequate substitute is a deep, heavy, seamless cake pan (with the same capacity as the mold called for in the recipe) covered tightly with a double thickness of heavy aluminum foil.

Teapots can be made of porcelain, glazed china, earthenware, silver, or just about any material except aluminum, which will turn the tea black.

Timers with a loud alarm are very helpful. Set it for a few minutes less than the minimum baking time suggested; it's better to get to the oven too soon than too late.

Toothpicks that are round and wooden are excellent for testing cakes and muffins for doneness. I find them more accurate than broom straws, wire testers, or skewers.

Wax paper is used to line cake pans, for rolling out pastry, and to transfer sifted dry ingredients.

Ingredients

♦

Baking powder and baking soda. These are not interchangeable. Baking powder is a leavener that reacts to liquid and heat by releasing carbon-dioxide bubbles, which expand during baking and cause dough to rise. Too much baking powder can cause an opposite effect: heavy, soggy batter that doesn't rise sufficiently. (Once a can of baking powder is opened its shelf life is only about three months, so replace it regularly.) Baking soda works in a similar way but is activated only when combined with certain ingredients, including buttermilk, sour milk, molasses (an ingredient in brown sugar), and honey.

Brown sugars. Light or dark brown sugar is specified in most recipes, but one can be exchanged for the other. It is the greater amount of molasses that gives dark brown sugar its strong flavor and dark color. To keep brown sugar soft, store it in a plastic bag in an airtight container.

Butter is the shortening of choice in cakes and cookies because its flavor is superior to any of the alternatives. I specify unsalted butter because I like the taste, but salted butter can be substituted; just be sure to omit any additional salt called for in the recipe. Health considerations may require substituting margarine. If so, use an unsalted variety.

Chocolate. Use the best quality available; you will be able to taste the difference. When melting chocolate, be slow and careful; it burns easily. Wrap chocolate for storage tightly; it absorbs odors. Use Dutch-processed cocoa in baking whenever possible, as it has been treated with a mild alkali to produce a smoother taste.

Coconut. I have a strong preference for unsweetened, shredded coconut because it doesn't taste of additives, as the sweetened varieties do. Unfortunately, it is difficult to find. Specialty-food shops may have unsweetened desiccated, or dried, coconut imported from Great Britain. Sweetened coconut can be rinsed in cold water to remove some of the sugar; it must be dried on several thicknesses of paper towels and then transferred to a shallow pan and dried further in a slow (warm) oven.

Cream cheese is made with varying proportions of gum additives, and when a brand name is specified it is because it is the only one that will produce the desired consistency.

Dried fruit. Only plump, moist raisins, apricots, and other dried fruits should be used in baking. Hard dried fruit will remain hard when baked in cakes and cookies. Apricots, raisins, and currants can be softened by soaking them in boiling water for a few minutes, draining them in a sieve, and drying them on several thicknesses of paper towels. Storing dried fruits at room temperature in self-sealing plastic bags will help to keep them soft.

Eggs. Most recipes call for eggs graded large. The size is specified in all recipes. Always break eggs into a cup or dish, not directly into other ingredients. If an egg is bad and contaminates the mixture, you will have to start from scratch.

If a recipe calls for separating eggs, do it while the eggs are cold, when they will separate more easily, then bring the yolks and whites to room temperature. Crack eggs on a flat surface rather than on the edge of a bowl; the shells will be less likely to splinter. If a bit of egg shell falls into the egg or if some yolk falls into the white, scoop it out with either a piece of an egg shell or the corner of a paper towel that has been dipped into cold water.

Never use a plastic bowl for beating egg whites because the plastic contains a chemical that inhibits expansion of the whites. Leftover egg whites can be stored, covered, in the refrigerator for up to three days. Leftover egg yolks can be stored in the refrigerator for up to three days in a tightly covered cup or small bowl with just enough water to cover them.

Extracts (vanilla and almond) are crucial to many recipes and only pure essence should be used. If artificial flavoring is all that is available, omit it.

Flour. Unbleached all-purpose flour was used in testing the recipes that follow, but bleached flour can be substituted, keeping in mind that it may produce baked goods that are lighter in color. Be careful not to overbake them while waiting for them to darken. Unless "sift before measuring" is indicated, recipes call for unsifted flour. Presifted flour will have to be resifted, as it settles on standing. Whole wheat flour, cake flour, self-rising cake flour, and bread flour are not interchangeable; use the type specified in each recipe. Weather conditions affect the amount of moisture flour can absorb, so be sure to add it to the batter gradually. Store flour in a cool, dry place; whole wheat flour should be refrigerated.

Nuts are perishable and become rancid if not stored tightly covered in a cold place: a few weeks in the refrigerator; up to a year in the freezer. If you are buying them loose, sniff them first; you will know if they are not fresh. Nuts frozen in their shells are easy to crack and extract.

Oatmeal. Use uncooked rolled oats: old-fashioned or quick-cooking are fine. Do not use instant oatmeal because it is absorbent and will become mushy when combined with wet ingredients. The longer the oats take to cook (check the directions on the package), the crunchier they will be in baked goods. I like to roast the oats for a short time to enhance their flavor before adding them, cooled, to dough.

Spices have a shelf life of about one year in most cases and should be replaced when they no longer smell pungent.

Sugar generally refers to white granulated sugar. While superfine or turbinado sugars can be substituted, they will yield baked goods that are either finer or coarser. Confectioners' sugar contains cornstarch and should be used in recipes only when specified.

Zest is the colored part of the rind of citrus fruits and is a key ingredient in many teatime foods. Avoid the white pith of the rind as it is bitter.

Techniques
◆

Read a recipe through to the end before beginning preparation; you might find you don't have enough time, or the proper pan, or a key ingredient.

Use the best quality ingredients available.

Assemble all required ingredients before you begin and set them aside as you use them so as not to omit any inadvertently.

Dust the inside of pan if a recipe calls for it by sprinkling flour or dry crumbs over the greased surface with your fingers or with a clean, unused powder puff; tap out the excess. The coating will cause the cake to shrink from the sides of the pan as it cools and will facilitate unmolding.

Soften butter by slicing it into many small pieces and placing it in a single layer on a flat plate at room temperature; do not melt it.

Cream butter and sugar by beating it slowly at first and then at medium speed until it is light in color and texture.

If using zest in a recipe, beat it in with the sugar, whose coarse granules will cause more flavor to be extracted from the rind.

Add ingredients in the order stated in the recipes; this is especially important with muffins and cornbread.

Pour batter evenly into the pan and smooth the top, or the result is likely to be a lopsided cake.

Use a mercury oven thermometer, allow 20 minutes for the oven to preheat, and check the temperature before placing the pan inside.

Set a timer for a few minutes less than the minimum time suggested and check the contents of the oven. If they are not ready, stick close to the oven and check frequently until they test done.

Do not open the oven door before three quarters of the suggested baking time has elapsed or the cake might fall. If your cake appears to be browning too quickly, cover it loosely with a sheet of aluminum foil during the latter part of the baking time.

Test cakes for doneness with a round wooden toothpick (I find them the only accurate utensil). Insert it deep into the center of the cake, or, for a tube cake, halfway between the tube and the edge, and draw it out slowly. If it comes out clean, with no uncooked batter on it (a bit of fruit or a speck of chopped nuts or a crumb might cling), it is done.

Do not be tempted to remove baked goods from their pans before the suggested cooling time; they will probably fall apart.

Proper Tea

◆

Bring fresh cold water to a boil in a kettle. Meanwhile, warm the teapot by rinsing it with hot water. Spoon 1 teaspoon of tea leaves for each person you wish to serve plus 1 for the pot into the warm teapot. If the water is left to boil, it will give up oxygen and the result will be bitter, muddy tea. Therefore, place the teapot near the kettle and as soon as the water begins to boil, pour it over the tea leaves. (Judge the amount of water by the size of your pot; i.e., if you have a 4-cup pot and are preparing tea for two, fill it halfway.) Stir once, cover the pot with the lid, and steep for 3½ to 5 minutes, depending on the strength desired. Strain the liquid into teacups and serve.

Once brewed to the desired strength, the tea should be poured at once or it will become bitter and unpleasant. If you wish to make enough for seconds or if you are having a tea party, steep the tea in one pot and strain it into a second, heated pot, where you can keep it warm under a cozy.

If you like milk in your tea, you may want to pour it into the empty cup first, as the English do. They believe, correctly I'm sure, that cool milk is unlikely to crack a fine teacup, while hot tea may. If you prefer lemon to milk, slice the fruit into thin rounds and remove the seeds. Sugar is added to taste.

Teabags are a fact of life, and a very convenient one at that. If you use them, follow the same basic rules:

warm the teapot or cup

use 1 teabag per person plus 1 for the pot

bring the pot or cup to the kettle

pour the water as soon as it boils

cover the pot or cup and steep for 3½ to 5 minutes

remove and discard the teabags

RECIPES

Pink Onion Tart

The color of this tart comes from the roasted red peppers, not the onions, which are white but are known as green onions or scallions. Actually, this is a variation of a classic quiche, particularly pretty and delicious. Served warm with a green salad, this would be just right for high tea, or, cut into small, thin wedges, as a savory for a lighter afternoon tea.

1 large red bell pepper
⅔ cup scallions, white part only
1 tablespoon butter
1 teaspoon water
1½ cups light cream
1 9-inch tart shell, lightly baked (recipe follows)

3 eggs, graded large
2 ounces (½ cup) mozzarella cheese, cut into ¼-inch cubes
2 tablespoons fresh basil leaves, washed, dried, and chopped
salt and freshly ground white pepper to taste

To roast the pepper: Place it in a shallow pan under a very hot broiler and turn it with tongs every few minutes until the skin is evenly blistered and charred in spots. Place the pepper in a brown paper bag or a heavy, self-sealing plastic bag and close securely. When the pepper has cooled, peel off the skin and cut away the core and seeds. Cut the pepper into small pieces and set aside.

Position an oven rack in the center of the oven and preheat the oven to 350 degrees.

Wash, dry, and trim the scallions and cut into thin rounds. Heat the butter in a medium skillet and add the scallions and water. Cook over medium-high heat, stirring constantly, for about 5 minutes until the water has evapo-

Pink Onion teapot, creamer, and sugar bowl: Japan 1950s

◆ *Pink Onion Tart*

◆ *Pâte Brisée (page 17)*

rated. Lower the heat to low, cover the pan, and cook about 10 minutes until the scallions are soft but not browned. Set aside to cool briefly.

Puree the chopped roasted pepper with ½ cup of the cream in a *food processor* or blender until smooth. Add the remaining cup of cream and the eggs and process briefly until just mixed; do not overprocess.

Set the tart shell (still in its pan) on a baking sheet. Spread the scallions evenly over the bottom of the pastry. Sprinkle the mozzarella and basil over the scallions. Add salt and white pepper to taste. Pour the pepper-cream-egg mixture over all and bake 30 to 40 minutes or until the point of a sharp knife inserted in the center comes out clean. Cool for 5 minutes before removing the rim of the pan. Leave the tart on the bottom of the pan; place a folded napkin on a serving plate (to keep the tart from sliding) and place the tart on the napkin. Serve warm.

Yield: 5 to 10 portions

High tea originated during the Industrial Revolution of the nineteenth century and was a meal favored by the working class in Great Britain, often consisting of leftovers or simple egg or cheese dishes. Today the term connotes an elaborate affair of the upper class. One thing hasn't changed: High tea is always served at the dining table to seated diners. Afternoon tea, occasionally called low tea, can be served anywhere in the home or garden.

Pâte Brisée
(Tart Shell or Pie Crust)

———◆———

This is an excellent, versatile dough. Add a bit of sugar for fruit pies, a pinch of dried herbs or spice for a savory shell; double the recipe for a 2-crust pie, halve the recipe for 2 small tarts. I find that when a recipe calls for a partially baked crust, it is better to err on the side of overbaking rather than under-baking. For the onion tart the shell should be almost completely baked, as it will not brown further (except at the very edges) once the filling is added. For this tart use a 9-inch quiche pan or tart pan with a fluted, removable rim.

1 cup plus 2 tablespoons unsifted all-
*   purpose flour*
pinch of salt
pinch of cayenne pepper (optional)

5 tablespoons unsalted butter, very cold
2 tablespoons solid vegetable shortening,
*   very cold*
2 to 3 tablespoons ice water

Combine the flour, salt, and pepper (if you are using it) in the work bowl of a *food processor.* Cut the cold butter into 1-inch cubes and add to the bowl along with the vegetable shortening. Pulse until the mixture looks like coarse meal. With the machine operating, dribble 2 tablespoons ice water through the feed tube and process until the dough comes together and forms a ball. If the dough remains crumbly, add a few drops of water until it forms a ball.

To prepare the dough *without a food processor:* Combine the flour, salt, and pepper (optional) in a large bowl. Cut the cold butter into ½-inch cubes and add to the bowl along with the vegetable shortening. Using a pastry blender or 2 table knives, cut in the butter and shortening until the mixture looks like coarse meal. Sprinkle ice water over the mixture and stir with a fork until a dough is formed. Turn out the dough onto a lightly floured surface and push off fistfuls of it with the heel of your hand until it is all smooth. Scrape the pushed off dough into a ball.

Wrap the ball of dough in plastic wrap and refrigerate for at least 30 minutes, or overnight if it is more convenient.

Place the chilled ball of dough on a lightly floured surface (or between large sheets of wax paper) and, if it is too firm to roll out, pound it with a floured rolling pin to soften it slightly. From the center outward, roll it into a circle about 11 inches in diameter. Lift the dough by rolling it loosely around the floured rolling pin and drape it onto the pan. Press the dough, without stretching it, into the pan and up the sides. Fold any excess dough down into the pan and press against the sides. The sides of the crust should be thicker than the bottom. Cover the dough with a piece of baking parchment or aluminum foil and refrigerate for at least 30 minutes.

When you are ready to bake, position an oven rack in the center of the oven and preheat the oven to 425 degrees.

Remove the parchment or foil and prick the dough all over (including the sides) with the tines of a fork. Replace the parchment in the shell and cover it completely with pie weights or uncooked rice or beans. Bake for 10 to 12 minutes until the edges begin to color. Remove the shell from the oven and gently remove the weight-filled parchment or foil. Return the shell to the oven and immediately reduce the oven temperature to 375 degrees. Bake 15 to 25 minutes or until the crust is golden brown all over. If the edges seem to be browning very fast, crimp a bit of aluminum foil over them. Remove from the oven and cool before filling.

Yield: 1 9-inch tart shell or bottom pie crust

> If you plan to prepare pie crust in warm weather (or if your kitchen is particularly warm), refrigerate all the ingredients——including the flour——and the pie tin for several hours before you begin.

Leek Toasts

◆

Although these toasts are more like Italian focaccia (pizza bread) than any Welsh snack I know, I've illustrated the recipe with my Welsh dresser teapot because I always associate leeks with Wales; they are, in fact, the national symbol of the country. Their mild, oniony flavor is just tangy enough for a teatime savory. These are simple to prepare and always well received.

2 to 3 medium leeks, white part only
    (about 2 cups sliced)
2 tablespoons butter
1 teaspoon water
¼ teaspoon granulated sugar
4 7-inch pita breads, pocketless if
    available

good-quality olive oil
fresh thyme leaves, chopped; or dried,
    crushed thyme
coarse salt

Trim the root ends of the leeks and remove the green parts. Slice the whites lengthwise and rinse under cold, running water, separating the layers to allow the water to wash away all traces of sand. Drain on a kitchen towel and slice crosswise into ¼-inch pieces.

Melt the butter in a medium, heavy skillet and add the leeks, water, and sugar. Cook over medium-high heat, stirring constantly, for about 5 minutes. Reduce the heat to low, cover the pan, and cook for 15 to 20 minutes until the leeks are soft and transparent but not browned.

Position an oven rack in the center of the oven and preheat the oven to 375 degrees.

Brush the tops of the pita breads with a few drops of olive oil. Cut each one into 6 wedges (like a pie). Spread about half a teaspoon of leeks on top of each triangle and sprinkle lightly (or to taste) with thyme and coarse salt. Place the triangles on a baking sheet and bake for about 10 minutes until the toasts are golden brown around the edges. Serve warm.

Yield: 24 small toasts

> *Savory* is the term given to dishes, cooked or uncooked, that are not sweet but piquant in flavor. Teatime savories include sandwiches, cheese dishes, herb toasts, and spicy crackers.

Welsh Dresser teapot: Swineside Ceramics Wensleydale, England 1980s

◆ *(left) Leek Toasts (page 19)*

◆ *(right) Welsh Cakes (page 22)*

Welsh Cakes

◆

How to describe a Welsh cake: not at all like a cake, somewhat like a scone or a biscuit, and baked like a pancake. While many people shy away from recipes that require rolling out dough, no one should be afraid of this one. The dough is easy to manage and forgiving. The Welsh name for these cakes translates to "cakes on the stone," indicating that they were originally cooked on a bakestone set over an open fire. I recommend a griddle.

2 cups unsifted all-purpose flour
1 tablespoon baking powder
pinch of salt
⅔ cup granulated sugar, divided
6 tablespoons (¾ stick) unsalted butter, very cold

2 tablespoons solid vegetable shortening, chilled
½ teaspoon grated lemon zest
1 egg, graded large, lightly beaten
2 to 4 teaspoons milk, as needed
½ cup currants or chopped raisins

Measure the flour, baking powder, salt, and sugar (reserve approximately 1 tablespoon of the sugar for decoration) into the work bowl of a *food processor* and pulse 2 or 3 times to combine. Add the butter, vegetable shortening, and lemon zest and pulse until the mixture looks like coarse meal. With the machine running, pour the beaten egg and 2 teaspoons of milk through the feed tube and process briefly until the mixture begins to come together. If after a few seconds the mixture looks dry, add a bit more milk a few drops at a time. Stop the machine and add the currants or raisins. Pulse once or twice to incorporate them. Do not overprocess.

To prepare *without a food processor:* In a large bowl stir together the flour, baking powder, and salt. Cut in the butter and shortening using a pastry blender or 2 table knives until the mixture looks like coarse meal. Add the sugar and lemon zest and combine. Beat in the egg and 2 teaspoons of milk, or a few drops more if the dough seems dry. Stir in the currants or raisins.

Turn the mixture out onto a floured surface, dust the top of it lightly with flour, knead it 3 or 4 times, and, with a floured rolling pin, roll the dough evenly to a ⅓-inch thickness. Using a round biscuit or cookie cutter 2 to 3 inches in diameter, cut out as many rounds as possible. Press the scraps together and cut out more rounds.

Heat a lightly greased griddle or large, heavy frying pan to low. It should be evenly heated and a drop of water should barely sizzle when sprinkled on it.

Cook as many of the cakes as your griddle will hold comfortably for 3 or 4 minutes on each side, turning each only once. The underside should be light brown before the cake is turned. If this happens too quickly, the griddle is too hot; reduce the heat. The cakes are done when both sides are light brown and the edges no longer look raw. Cool the cakes on a wire rack and sprinkle with sugar before serving with tea. Store in the freezer; reheat on a baking sheet in a preheated 350-degree oven for approximately 10 minutes to defrost.

Yield: 14 to 18 small cakes

Overdry raisins, currants, etc., can——and should——be plumped in boiling water for a few minutes, drained, and dried on several thicknesses of paper toweling before being added to cake or cookie batter. If not, they may become even harder when baked.

Scottish Scones

Everything about the scone seems to be touched with controversy: the derivation of the word (Gaelic or Dutch?), the pronunciation of the word (does it rhyme with *bone* or *gone*?), its shape (round, triangular, or square?), its toppings (should the cream—Devonshire or whipped?—be spread directly on the split scone or dropped on top of the strawberry jam?), and on and on. However, there does seem to be general agreement that scones are a staple on the teatime menu. When served fresh from the oven, they are delicious even without the addition of butter, cream, jam, or honey. A crumbly, yet moist not flaky, texture is the goal when baking scones and it is best achieved by handling the dough as little as possible.

2 cups unsifted all-purpose flour
1¾ teaspoons baking powder
½ teaspoon baking soda
pinch of salt
¼ cup granulated sugar
½ cup (1 stick) unsalted butter, soft
   (not melted)

½ cup currants (optional)
⅔ cup buttermilk
1 teaspoon grated orange rind (zest)

Optional glaze:
2 tablespoons milk or heavy cream or
   1 egg, lightly beaten

Sift together the flour, baking powder, baking soda, and salt twice. In a large bowl mix the sifted ingredients with the sugar. Cut in the butter with a pastry blender or 2 knives until the mixture looks like fresh bread crumbs or coarse meal. (A *food processor* can be used up to this point but not beyond. Turn the mixture into a large bowl and continue.) If you are using currants, add them and stir to distribute them. Cover the bowl with plastic wrap and refrigerate for at least 15 minutes, and at most 24 hours.

 Scotty the Golfer teapot: Wade Ceramics Staffordshire, England 1950s

◆ *(left) Scottish Scones*

◆ *(right) Scotch Oatmeal Raisin Cookies (page 27)*

Position an oven rack in the top of the oven and preheat the oven to 425 degrees. If you are making round or triangular scones, place an ungreased baking sheet in the oven to heat. If you are making square scones, lightly flour a baking sheet and set it aside. Do not preheat it.

Remove the butter-flour mixture from the refrigerator and make a well in the center. Measure the buttermilk, mix in the orange zest, and pour into the well. Stir with a fork until a soft, somewhat sticky dough is formed. Now it is important to work quickly because once the liquid is combined with the dry ingredients, the leavening action begins.

To make *Round Scones:* Turn the dough out onto a lightly floured board or other surface and with floured hands gently knead it 12 times. Pat the mass to an even ¾-inch thickness. With a sharp 2-inch round cutter, cut out as many rounds as possible. Do not twist the cutter into the dough or it will bake lopsided. Just press straight down to cut through the dough. Use a metal spatula to transfer the scones to the preheated baking sheet, placing them 1 inch apart. Gently, but quickly, press together the scraps of dough and cut out more scones. If you want the scones to have a shiny top, brush them lightly with cream or egg. Bake in the top of the oven for 12 to 14 minutes or until they have risen to about twice their height, are golden brown on top, and are firm to the touch.

To make *Triangular Scones:* Turn the dough out onto a lightly floured board or other surface and with floured hands gently knead it 12 times. Pat the dough into 2 even rounds about ¾ inch thick. With a sharp knife cut each round into 6 wedges. Transfer them with a metal spatula to the preheated baking sheet, placing them 1 inch apart. Brush on glaze if desired. Bake in the top of the oven for 10 to 13 minutes or until they have risen to about twice their height, are golden brown on top, and are firm to the touch.

To make *Square Scones:* These are handled least and, therefore, are the lightest in texture. Unfortunately, they are not the prettiest to look at. Your choice. Do not preheat the baking sheet. Turn out the dough onto the floured baking sheet and with floured hands pat it into a ¾-inch-thick rectangle. With a sharp knife cut 12 even squares and gently move them about 1 inch apart on the baking sheet. Glaze if desired. Bake 12 to 15 minutes or until they have risen to about twice their height, are golden brown on top, and are firm to the touch.

Transfer the scones to a wire rack to cool for 5 minutes. Serve warm. Scones can be frozen. When cool, wrap them airtight in a plastic bag and freeze for up to 1 month. Reheat them, frozen, on a baking sheet in a preheated 350-degree oven for about 10 minutes.

Yield: 12 scones

NOTE: To make *brown scones,* use 1½ cups whole wheat flour and ½ cup all-purpose flour; all other ingredients are the same.

An unusual and delicious substitute for Devonshire cream (the traditional spread for scones) is the creamy, rich Italian cheese mascarpone.

Scotch Oatmeal Raisin Cookies

◆

If you like your oatmeal cookies light and crisp, these are for you. The *Scotch* in the title refers to the whiskey in the recipe, and can be replaced with vanilla extract if you prefer. Be sure the raisins you use are soft because they will not soften as they bake in the cookies; they might even get harder. To plump raisins, simply put them in a heat-proof bowl, pour boiling water over them, and let them steep for 3 to 5 minutes. Drain, then dry them with several thicknesses of paper towels.

1½ cups old-fashioned rolled oats (not instant)
¾ cup unsifted all-purpose flour
½ teaspoon baking soda
pinch of salt
½ cup (1 stick) unsalted butter, softened
½ cup light brown sugar, firmly packed

⅓ cup granulated sugar
1 egg, graded large
1 teaspoon Scotch whiskey (or pure vanilla extract)
½ cup soft raisins
½ cup walnuts, chopped into raisin-size pieces

Position 2 oven racks to divide the oven into thirds and preheat the oven to 350 degrees. Line cookie sheets with baking parchment or aluminum foil, shiny side up.

Place the uncooked oatmeal in a baking pan at least 9 inches by 13 inches by 1½ inches and bake in the preheated oven for 20 minutes, stirring every few minutes to toast the oats evenly. Set aside to cool.

Sift the flour, soda, and salt together and set aside. Cream the butter with both sugars until fluffy. Add the egg and whiskey (or vanilla extract) and mix until combined. Mix in the cooled oats, then the flour mixture, stirring only until just incorporated. Stir in the raisins and walnuts.

Using a measuring teaspoon and a tiny rubber spatula, drop the dough onto the lined cookie sheets by rounded teaspoonfuls about 2 inches apart. Bake 2 sheets at a time for 13 to 15 minutes or until the cookies are golden brown all over. Rotate the sheets front to back and top to bottom after 7 minutes to ensure even baking. Allow the cookies to rest on the parchment or foil for a minute or so before transferring them with a metal spatula to wire racks to cool completely. Store airtight to retain crispness.

Yield: 4 to 5 dozen 2-inch cookies

> Roasting oats in a moderate oven for 10 to 15 minutes (stirring occasionally) will enhance their flavor in baked goods.

Pig's Ears

◆

Also known as *palmiers,* these flaky pastries are an elegant addition to the tea table. Decent commercial puff pastry is readily available in supermarkets, so these can be made quickly and easily at home. They are best when freshly baked; I recommend making a small batch unless you are feeding a crowd.

granulated sugar

1 sheet (about ½ pound) frozen puff pastry, thawed

You will need a large, clean, dry board or work surface to roll out the pastry. Sprinkle the surface thickly and evenly with sugar. Place the pastry (it should be pliable but cold) on the sugar and sprinkle additional sugar evenly over the top. With a rolling pin roll it about ⅛ inch thick, keeping the shape square. Using a plastic ruler as a guide, trim the edges with a sharp knife.

To achieve the classic pig's ear shape, you will have to fold the pastry in on itself. This sounds more difficult than it is: measure the square of pastry to determine where the exact center is and vertically mark it lightly with the edge of the ruler. Fold half the pastry 2 turns toward the center (the first turn will be ⅓ of the half, the second turn will be ⅔) so that the folded edge is almost, but not quite, at the center mark. Repeat with the other side. The pastry will look like a flattened scroll. The final fold is to close the two rolled halves together like a book. Now you have a long, thin roll of 6 thicknesses of pastry. Wrap the roll in plastic wrap and refrigerate it for 30 minutes to 1 hour.

Position an oven rack in the center of the oven and preheat the oven to 400 degrees. Line a cookie sheet with aluminum foil, shiny side up.

Remove the pastry from the refrigerator and, using a very sharp knife, cut it into slices about ½ inch thick. Sprinkle both cut sides of each slice with sugar. Place the "ears" 2 to 3 inches apart on the lined cookie sheet. You will probably have room for only half the ears on one sheet. Place the balance on another sheet of aluminum foil and set aside. Bake one sheet at a time in the center of the oven for 10 to 13 minutes until the cookies are puffed up and are sitting in a little pool of golden brown sugar-syrup. Remove the cookie sheet and, working quickly with tongs or 2 metal spatulas, turn the cookies over. Return to the oven for 2 or 3 minutes until the tops are golden brown. Remove the cookie sheet from the oven and immediately slide the foil onto a flat surface. Slide the sheet (it doesn't matter if it is hot) under the foil with the unbaked "ears" and bake them. Transfer the baked cookies to a wire rack. They should be very crisp when cool. Store in an airtight container.

Yield: 18 to 24 2-inch cookies

Bacon and Avocado Sandwiches

Except for the bacon, there is nothing piggy about these; they're delicate in both taste and size. Because avocado discolors quickly, the sandwiches should be made shortly before you plan to serve them.

4 slices bacon
2 tablespoons unsalted butter, softened
2 tablespoons mayonnaise
few drops Worcestershire sauce
few drops hot pepper sauce
freshly ground black pepper, to taste

8 to 10 slices very *thinly sliced white bread (Pepperidge Farm Very Thin is excellent)*
1 large, ripe avocado (the flesh should yield to slight pressure but not feel soft)
½ teaspoon lemon juice, freshly squeezed

Cut the bacon into 1-inch pieces and fry until crisp, stopping to pour off the fat as it accumulates. Drain the bacon on paper towels. When thoroughly cool, chop it finely and set aside.

In a small bowl combine the butter, mayonnaise, Worcestershire sauce, hot pepper sauce, and black pepper. Working quickly (the bread dries out quickly when exposed to the air), spread one side of each slice of bread with the mixture. Peel and thinly slice the avocado and sprinkle it with the lemon juice. Place the avocado slices on half the bread, sprinkle the chopped bacon over the avocado, and cover with the remaining bread, buttered side down. With a sharp knife trim the crusts on all sides, making even squares with clean edges, and cut the sandwiches diagonally into 4 triangles each. Serve at once. (The bread will dry out very quickly, so cover the sandwiches with damp paper towels if they have to stand for more than a few minutes.)

Yield: 16 to 20 tiny sandwiches

Cream tea refers to a late-afternoon meal of tiny sandwiches, scones with Devonshire or whipped cream and preserves, rich cake or tarts, and, of course, tea. It does not refer to an alternative to milk or lemon in hot tea.

For centuries tea was used as currency in Asia. The leaves were steamed, pounded, placed in molds, and baked to form a brick. The tea bricks were the currency, and bits that fell from them were used to brew the beverage.

Savory Corn Muffins

◆

If you have fresh corn, by all means cut the kernels from one or two ears and use it to make muffins. However, frozen corn works perfectly well in this recipe and you can make it anytime. These sunny, yellow "confetti" muffins have a dark, buttery bottom "crust" and are fabulous served warm with hot pepper jelly—and tea, of course.

½ cup frozen corn kernels, thawed
6 tablespoons (¾ stick) unsalted butter,
melted and cooled, plus additional
butter for pans
¼ cup onion, finely chopped
1 cup unsifted all-purpose flour
1 cup yellow cornmeal
1 tablespoon baking powder
2 tablespoons granulated sugar

½ teaspoon salt
2 eggs, graded large
1 cup less 1 tablespoon milk, at room
temperature
2 tablespoons red bell pepper, seeded and
finely chopped
1 tablespoon jalapeño pepper, seeded and
finely chopped

Position an oven rack in the center of the oven and preheat the oven to 400 degrees. Heavily butter 15 muffin cups (even if they have a nonstick surface) with unsalted butter. This will result in a dark, crusty bottom on the muffins as well as provide a "release" on the muffin pans. Set aside.

Spread the thawed kernels of corn in a single layer on a kitchen towel or a double thickness of paper towels to absorb the excess moisture. Set aside.

Combine 1 teaspoon of the melted butter and the chopped onion in a small nonstick skillet over low heat, cover tightly, and "sweat" for 10 to 15 min-

Corn teapot: probably Japan 1950s

◆ *(left) Pineapple Cornmeal Skillet Cake (page 37)*

◆ *(right) Savory Corn Muffins*

utes, stirring occasionally, until the onions are soft and transparent but not browned. Set aside to cool.

In a large bowl stir and toss the flour, cornmeal, baking powder, sugar, and salt together to distribute the ingredients evenly.

Place the buttered muffin pans in the heated oven for a few minutes until they are hot. Remove them from the oven and prepare the muffins, working quickly to complete the batter while the pans are still warm.

In a medium bowl beat the eggs, milk, and the remaining melted butter until combined. Stir in the corn, onions, and peppers. Pour this mixture over the dry ingredients and gently fold just until incorporated and no flour is visible. Spoon into the muffin cups, filling each about ⅔ full. Bake for 20 to 25 minutes until the muffins are firm to the touch and a wooden tooth-pick inserted in the center of a muffin comes out clean. The tops will not color much except at the edges. Remove from the oven and allow the muffins to rest in the pans for 5 minutes before turning them out onto a rack. Serve them warm. Once cooled (or frozen), they can be reheated in a preheated 350-degree oven.

Yield: 15 2½-inch muffins

Use foil baking cups set on a small baking sheet or upside-down pie tin if there is only a small amount of batter left in the bowl. Don't be tempted to overfill muffin cups to "come out even."

Pineapple Cornmeal Skillet Cake

◆

When I was a college student in Virginia, I was first introduced to this unusual form of cornbread. Because it was always offered with iced tea, I think of it as a tea cake, and a delicious one at that. Prepared like a syrupy upside-down cake, this is quick and easy. Serve it shortly after it comes out of the oven, slightly warm, or at room temperature.

½ cup (1 stick) unsalted butter, divided
¼ cup light brown sugar, firmly packed
1 tablespoon dark corn syrup
1 8-ounce can unsweetened crushed pineapple, drained
½ cup plus 2 tablespoons yellow cornmeal

½ cup plus 2 tablespoons unsifted all-purpose flour
3 tablespoons granulated sugar
2 teaspoons baking powder
pinch of salt
1 egg, graded large
¾ cup milk, at room temperature

Position a rack in the center of the oven and preheat the oven to 425 degrees. You will need a heavy skillet that is oven-proof (does not have a wooden handle) and is about 8 inches in diameter. If your skillet has slanted sides and is smaller on the bottom and larger on the top, check its capacity by pouring measured cups of water into it. If it holds between 5 and 6 cups, it is fine. Over low heat melt 3 tablespoons of the butter in the skillet. Swirl the butter around the skillet to grease the sides thoroughly. Add the brown sugar and dark corn syrup. Increase the heat to medium and cook, stirring, until the mixture begins to boil. Remove the skillet from the heat and smooth the mixture with the back of a spoon so that it is evenly distributed in the skillet. Spoon the drained pineapple evenly over the butter and sugar. Set aside.

In a small bowl combine the cornmeal, flour, granulated sugar, baking powder, and salt. Stir with a fork until blended. Set aside.

In a medium bowl cream the remaining 5 tablespoons butter, which should be soft, until smooth. Add the egg and milk and beat until blended. Pour in the combined dry ingredients and stir until they are just incorporated. Do not overmix. Pour the batter into the prepared skillet, covering the pineapple evenly. Bake for 20 to 25 minutes until the center of the cake springs back when gently touched and a wooden toothpick inserted partway into the center comes out clean. The syrup should be dark and bubbling up at the edges. Remove the skillet from the oven and place it over medium-high heat for 1 minute to caramelize the pineapple further. Remove the skillet from the heat and allow it to rest for 2 minutes. Cover the skillet with a flat serving plate and invert them so that the skillet is on top. Remove the skillet. Scrape out any pineapple and syrup that remain in the skillet and replace it on the cake. While the cake is delicious when slightly warm, it should not be served hot; syrup burns are no fun!

Yield: 6 portions

Teas with a medium-strong flavor, such as Kenya, black currant, orange pekoe, and Formosa oolong, are appropriate with the hot dishes associated with high tea. Delicate (e.g., Keemun, Earl Grey) and fruit-flavored teas are better with the mild-flavored foods served at afternoon tea. So-called "breakfast tea" is blended with high-caffeine varieties and is considered too brisk to serve later in the day.

Humpty Dumpty Egg and Cheese Tart

This is a typical high tea dish: staple ingredients, easy to prepare, and light enough to allow room for the sweets to follow. The British would use a short pastry crust, but I think the bread base is a lighter, and better, alternative.

9 to 12 slices fresh whole wheat or white bread
10 ounces (2½ cups, loosely packed) grated Cheddar cheese or Monterey Jack cheese

6 eggs
hot red pepper sauce, to taste
2½ tablespoons milk
1 tablespoon butter, plus additional butter for pan

Position an oven rack in the center of the oven and preheat the oven to 425 degrees. Generously butter the bottom and sides of a 9-inch tart pan with a removable, fluted rim.

Remove and reserve the crusts from the bread slices. Fit the slices into the prepared pan, overlapping them by at least ½ inch (the bread will shrink when baked). If necessary, cut some of the slices into smaller pieces in order to cover the pan completely. With your fingertips, press the bread, which

should be soft, into the pan, pushing it flat against the bottom and into the sides of the rim. Make sure there are no uncovered spots. Bake the bread in the center of the oven for 7 to 10 minutes until the center looks lightly toasted. If the edges brown too quickly, crimp strips of aluminum foil over them to keep them from burning. Remove the pan from the oven and reduce the oven temperature to 350 degrees. Allow the "crust" to cool for 5 minutes or so on a rack.

Using a *food processor* or standing grater, grate the reserved bread crusts into fine bread crumbs. Set aside.

Place half the cheese evenly over the toasted bread in the pan. Using the back of a tablespoon, depress 6 hollows into the cheese. Carefully break an egg into each hollow. Cover the eggs with the remaining cheese. Sprinkle 6 tablespoons bread crumbs evenly over all. Mix a few drops of hot pepper sauce into the milk and dribble it over the bread crumbs. Cut the butter into bits and dot the top of the tart with them.

Make sure the oven temperature has reached 350 degrees. Bake the tart for 20 to 35 minutes (depending on the size and temperature of the eggs you have used) until the filling is just set. After 20 minutes gently push the pan. If the filling jiggles only slightly and the egg whites look set (some will probably be visible), it is ready. Remove the tart from the oven and set on a rack to cool for 2 or 3 minutes. Carefully remove the rim; you may have to pry it loose with the point of a knife if the cheese has run over at some places. Leave the tart on the bottom of the pan and place it on a folded napkin (to keep it from sliding) on a flat plate. Serve at once.

Yield: 6 servings

Humpty Dumpty teapot: Lingard Pottery England 1930s

◆ *(left) Humpty Dumpty Egg and Cheese Tart (page 39)*

◆ *(right) Smoked Salmon–Stuffed Eggs (page 42)*

Smoked Salmon-Stuffed Eggs

Once considered the perfect food, eggs have been reclassified as a food to eat only occasionally because of their high cholesterol content. With that in mind, I've cut back on the "offending" yolks. The taste and texture are barely affected and the result is a near-perfect teatime savory.

6 eggs, at room temperature
4 ounces smoked salmon, finely chopped
1 tablespoon lemon juice, freshly squeezed
1 tablespoon finely snipped dill

1 tablespoon finely chopped chives
freshly ground pepper, to taste
1 tablespoon no-fat plain yogurt
1 tablespoon mayonnaise
chives or dill for decoration

Bring enough water to cover the eggs to a boil in a medium saucepan. Reduce the heat so that the water is boiling gently, not furiously. Pierce the round end of each egg with a straight pin (to prevent the shells from cracking) and gently lower the eggs into the boiling water. Simmer for 15 minutes. Have a large bowl of ice water ready, and as soon as the eggs are cooked, drain them and plunge them into the ice water.

When the eggs are cool to the touch, peel them and halve them lengthwise. Remove the yolks carefully and discard 2 (4 halves). Force the remaining yolks through a sieve into a medium bowl. With a fork, stir in the remaining ingredients until combined. To make the egg whites sit flat on a plate, slice a tiny bit off the bottom of each. Spoon a generous mound of salmon-yolk filling into each egg half. Place a bit of dill or chives on each. Cover securely with plastic wrap and refrigerate if you are not serving the eggs at once.

Yield: 12 portions

> If you have stored hard-cooked eggs and raw eggs together and are not sure which is which, twirl them on their pointed ends; the raw eggs will fall over and the cooked ones will spin.

Duck Sandwiches

◆

Tea sandwiches are traditionally small, thin, soft, and mild-flavored. However, they don't have to be tasteless and gummy. Using many of the elements of exotic Chinese Peking duck, these little sandwiches are perfectly appropriate for a "proper tea." (If you don't happen to have a roast duck, try smoked turkey or smoked chicken.) Brew a Chinese black tea, such as Keemun, or a semifermented oolong to go with the sandwiches.

½ firm cucumber
¼ cup scallion (green part only), minced
6 tablespoons (¾ stick) unsalted butter, softened
1 unsliced sandwich loaf, very fresh and soft

⅓ pound roast duck breast or smoked chicken or smoked turkey, sliced thin
hoisin sauce ("Chinese ketchup," available in Chinese groceries and specialty-food shops)

Peel the cucumber and cut in half lengthwise. Using the pointed top of a teaspoon, scrape out the seeds and discard them. Chop the flesh into tiny (¼-inch or smaller) cubes; measure ⅓ cup and spread on several thicknesses of paper towels to remove as much moisture as possible. Wrap the cubes in dry paper towels and refrigerate for 30 minutes.

Combine the cubed cucumber, minced scallion greens, and softened butter in a small bowl and set aside.

Use a sharp knife to cut the crusts from the loaf of bread. Slice the loaf the long way, making at least 4 uniform pieces, each at least ½ inch thick. Use a rolling pin to flatten the slices until they are very thin. Cover the flattened bread with damp paper towels to keep it from becoming dry while you assemble the sandwiches.

Working with 1 slice of bread at a time, thoroughly spread it with the butter mixture. Cover with thin slices of poultry, leaving a 1-inch margin at one short end of the bread. Stir the hoisin sauce until it is smooth and dab about a half-teaspoonful onto the poultry. Roll the bread like a jelly roll toward the end with the butter-only margin. Wrap the roll tightly in plastic wrap and continue to assemble and wrap the remaining sandwiches. Refrigerate them for at least 30 minutes. Cut each roll into ¾-inch pinwheels, arrange on a serving plate, cover with damp paper towels, and bring to room temperature before serving.

Yield: approximately 24 small sandwiches

(left) Duck teapot from Old MacDonald's Farm series: Regal China Antioch, Illinois 1950s

(right) Mabel Lucie Attwell Duck teapot: Shelley Pottery England 1930s

(left) Cheese Quackers (page 46)

(right) Duck Sandwiches (page 43)

Cheese Quackers

A plate of savory crackers like these is a lovely addition to the tea table. The dough puffs up slightly during baking to create little pillows. They're light, have a tangy flavor, and can be made quickly in a *food processor.*

1 cup unsifted all-purpose flour
pinch of salt
pinch of cayenne pepper
pinch of dry mustard
4 ounces sharp Cheddar cheese (cubed, approximately 1 cup)

¼ cup (½ stick) unsalted butter, frozen or very cold
1 egg yolk, graded large
toasted sesame, cumin, or caraway seeds (optional)

Position 2 oven racks to divide the oven into thirds and preheat the oven to 400 degrees. Line cookie sheets with baking parchment or aluminum foil, shiny side up, and set aside.

Place the flour, salt, cayenne, and dry mustard in the work bowl of a *food processor* and pulse 2 or 3 times just to mix. Dice the cheese and the butter into ½-inch cubes and add. Pulse until the mixture looks like coarse meal.

Stop the machine, add the yolk, and process until the dough begins to form a ball. Do not overmix.

Scrape half the dough onto a sheet of wax paper and pat it into a flat disk. Wrap securely and refrigerate while you work with the remaining dough. Scrape it onto a large sheet of wax paper, pat it into a disk, and cover it with another large sheet of wax paper. With a rolling pin, roll the dough—still between the wax paper—into a rectangle approximately ¼ inch thick. Lift and replace the top and bottom wax paper as often as necessary to smooth any wrinkles that result from rolling. Slide the "package" onto a cutting board or cookie sheet and place it in the freezer for 5 to 10 minutes while you roll out the rest of the dough. Remove the chilled dough from the freezer and lift and lightly replace the top paper. Invert and remove the paper that is now on top. With a pastry wheel, pizza cutter, or sharp knife, cut the dough into 1-inch (or slightly larger) squares. You may want to use a plastic ruler as a guide; just lay it lightly on the dough and cut on either side of the ruler. Use a small metal spatula to transfer the squares to the prepared cookie sheets. Place them about 1½ inches apart. Refrigerate the squares while you cut the rest of the dough. If desired, sprinkle a few seeds on top of each square.

Bake 2 sheets at a time for 10 to 15 minutes or until the pillows have puffed slightly and are barely colored at the edges. Allow them to rest on the parchment or foil for a minute or two before transferring them with a metal spatula to a wire rack to cool completely. Store them in an airtight tin for up to 1 week.

Yield: 4 dozen bite-size crackers

Honeymoon Sandwiches

These simple but delicious sandwiches get their name from the singular filling: lettuce alone, as in "Let us alone—we're on our honeymoon." They are delicate in both appearance and flavor. Be sure to use only the tender inner leaves of the lettuce.

fresh chives
12 slices soft, very thinly sliced bread (Pepperidge Farm Very Thin is excellent)
1 tablespoon minced fresh herbs such as basil or parsley

3 to 4 tablespoons unsalted butter, softened
12 inner leaves from 1 head curly leaf lettuce, washed and dried

Bride and Groom teapot: Laura Wilensky Kingston, New York 1993

♦ *(left) Groom's Cake (page 50)*

♦ *(right) Honeymoon Sandwiches*

Blanch 12 long, thin chive leaves in a skillet of boiling water for a few seconds until they become limp. Drain on a towel and set aside.

Trim the crusts from the bread and roll the slices with a rolling pin until they are flat. Cover the bread with damp paper towels to keep it from drying out while you assemble the sandwiches.

Stir the minced herbs into the butter and spread some evenly over 1 slice of flattened bread (keeping the others covered). Fold (don't cut or break) a lettuce leaf to fit on the bread, with the curly edge extending over one edge of the bread. Roll it like a jelly roll and tie it with a chive leaf. Trim the chive leaf and immediately cover the sandwich with a damp paper towel to keep it from drying out. Continue assembling the sandwiches, covering each as it is completed. Serve at once.

Yield: 12 small sandwiches

> A delightful punch can be made by mixing 2 parts champagne with 1 part iced tea. Garnish with fresh fruit and top off each glass with a bit of champagne from the bottle.

Groom's Cake
(Spiced Fruitcake)

Occasionally at weddings the guests are given small, beautifully wrapped slices of fruitcake to take home; this is the groom's cake. I tracked down the recipe (for 60 portions) of a particularly good one I'd been given at a wedding several years ago and reduced it to yield a tiny, round tea cake. It is moist and flavorful, as fruitcakes can be if the best quality fruits, nuts, and brandy are used, but the recipe is not original to the caterer who shared it with me; a similar one can be found in *The Fannie Farmer Baking Book*.

♦♦♦

*2½ cups dried fruit cut into 1-inch pieces
(see Note)*
*1½ cups nuts broken into large pieces
(see Note)*
*grated rind (zest) of 1 dark-skinned
orange*
1 teaspoon powdered spices (see Note)
*1 tablespoon dark corn syrup or golden
syrup or molasses*
*⅔ cup fruit juice or rum or brandy (see
Note)*

1 cup unsifted all-purpose flour
¾ teaspoon baking powder
½ teaspoon baking soda
pinch of salt
½ cup (1 stick) unsalted butter, softened
¾ cup light brown sugar, firmly packed
2 eggs, graded large
1 teaspoon pure vanilla extract

NOTE: Use any and all dried fruits and nuts that you like and none that you don't like. Virtually any combination works. If you love apricots and walnuts, try them exclusively, *or* try ½ cup *each* pitted dates, currants, golden raisins, apricots, and pitted prunes with ½ cup *each* almonds, pecans, and walnuts.

The same is true of the powdered spices. I like ½ teaspoon cinnamon, ¼ teaspoon cloves, and a pinch *each* allspice and freshly grated nutmeg.

For the liquid ingredients it is important to use the best, i.e., freshly squeezed orange juice or good-quality rum or brandy. I don't much care for teatime foods that taste strongly of alcohol, so I use the juice of 1 orange, 1 tablespoon Grand Marnier orange liqueur, and white grape juice to make a total of ⅔ cup.

As for the syrup, only 1 tablespoon is needed and it will affect the taste of the cake very little. Use whichever you have on hand.

Combine the dried fruit, nuts, orange zest, and powdered spices in a large bowl. In a small bowl or measuring cup combine the syrup and fruit juice

♦♦♦

and/or liqueur and pour the mixture over the fruit and nuts. Toss to combine and set aside for at least 1 hour or overnight, if it is more convenient.

When you are ready to bake, position an oven rack in the center of the oven and preheat the oven to 275 degrees. Use butter or no-stick cooking spray to grease 2 6-inch round baking pans (or 1 9-inch-by-5-inch loaf pan). Cut baking parchment or wax paper to line the bottoms of the pans, place paper in the pans, grease it thoroughly, then dust with flour. Tap out the excess and set aside.

Measure the flour, baking powder, baking soda, and salt into a medium bowl or onto a sheet of wax paper and stir to combine. Set aside.

Using an electric mixer, cream the butter and brown sugar together until fluffy. Add the eggs, one at a time, and the vanilla extract, stopping to scrape the sides of the bowl once or twice. Stir in the dry ingredients slowly but thoroughly. Pour and scrape the batter over the fruit-and-nut mixture and fold until incorporated. Spoon into the prepared pans and place them in the oven on the same shelf but not touching each other. Bake for about 2 hours until the cakes begin to shrink from the sides of the pans and a wooden toothpick inserted into the center of each comes out clean, with no uncooked batter on it. Place the pans on wire racks to cool for about 30 minutes, then turn out the cakes, carefully peel off the paper, and invert onto wire racks to continue cooling right side up. They can be served the day they are baked or a month later, improving with age. To store, wrap each cake securely in plastic wrap and foil and refrigerate. Slice when cold.

Yield: 2 6-inch rounds or 1 9-inch loaf

Chocolate Steamed Pudding

◆

While most steamed puddings are more appropriate for dessert than for tea, this pound cake–like pudding is an excellent teatime confection. It is divine when hot, delectable served warm, and delightful at room temperature. Although the recipe calls for a considerable amount of rum, 2 hours in the steamer leaves only a trace of alcohol and a hint of rum flavor. *You will need a 1½-quart steamed-pudding mold with a tight-fitting lid. (See Equipment, page 4.)*

3 ounces semisweet chocolate
1 cup plus 2 tablespoons unsifted all-
    purpose flour
1 tablespoon unsweetened cocoa powder,
    preferably Dutch-processed
1½ teaspoons baking powder
½ teaspoon pure vanilla extract
1 cup soft, fresh, unflavored bread
    crumbs, loosely packed
¾ cup (1½ sticks) unsalted butter plus
    butter for mold and wax paper
¾ cup granulated sugar plus sugar for
    mold

pinch of salt
1 tablespoon instant-coffee or espresso
    powder
1 tablespoon hot water
¼ cup milk
¼ cup dark rum
3 eggs, graded large
sweetened whipped cream or sour cream
    sauce (see page 59) as an
    accompaniment

Heavily butter the pudding mold and sprinkle the buttered surface with sugar. Tap out the excess. Using the lid as a guide, cut out a round of wax paper that will just fit the top of the mold. Butter one side of the paper and set aside. You will need a stock pot or kettle large enough to enclose the mold, and a metal rack or ring from a mason jar lid. Put a few inches of water to boil in the stock pot and put up a kettle to boil. (You'll need to add boiling water to the pot after you put in the mold.)

Heat the chocolate in a double boiler over hot water or in a microwave oven until it is mostly melted. Remove from the heat and stir until it is completely melted and smooth. Set it aside to cool slightly.

Onto a large piece of wax paper sift the flour, cocoa powder, baking powder, and salt. Set aside.

Dissolve the coffee powder in the hot water and combine with the milk, rum, and vanilla extract. Place the bread crumbs in a medium bowl and pour the coffee-rum mixture over them. Stir to blend. Set aside.

With an electric mixer, cream the butter and sugar until light and fluffy. Add the eggs, one at a time, beating to incorporate after each addition. Add the melted chocolate and beat to combine. Add the bread crumb mixture and beat at low speed, scraping the sides of the bowl as necessary. Stir in the dry ingredients and beat at lowest speed until smooth. Pour and scrape the batter into the prepared mold and smooth the top. Cover the mold with the wax paper round, butter side down, and the lid. Put the rack or mason jar ring in the stock pot (use long tongs or a wooden spoon to position it in the center), set the mold on the ring, and pour in boiling water to reach two thirds of the way up the mold; return the water to a boil. Cover the stock pot and simmer on very low heat for 2 hours.

Radiator teapot: Swineside Ceramics Wensleydale, England 1990

◆ *(left) Chocolate Steamed Pudding (page 53)*

◆ *(right) Figgy Steamed Pudding (page 57)*

Remove the mold from the stock pot, wipe the lid, and carefully remove it and the paper. Allow the pudding to cool for 5 minutes before turning it out onto a serving plate. Serve hot, warm, or at room temperature with whipped cream or sour cream sauce, if desired.

Yield: 6 to 8 portions

To avoid burned chocolate, melt it very slowly and remove it from the source of heat while there are still solid pieces of chocolate visible. Stir frequently.

Americans tend to think of tea drinking as British in origin, but several countries have longer histories of the custom: China and Japan in the sixth and eighth centuries, respectively, Holland at the beginning of the seventeenth century, Portugal shortly afterward, and, finally, England circa 1650. It was almost two hundred years before Indian tea plantations were developed by——and for——the British.

Figgy Steamed Pudding

◆

Every year for eight years at the Ethical Culture School Christmas assembly I heard my son and daughter and their schoolmates sing, "We all want some figgy pudding . . ." They didn't know what figgy pudding was and could only guess why they might have wanted it. Well, it's not pudding as we know it, but more like a light and delicately flavored cake and an ideal treat to serve at a holiday tea. It is best eaten just after it is unmolded, while it is still hot. It tends to sink slightly when cool but is still delicious. *To make it you will need a 1½-quart steamed-pudding mold with a tight-fitting lid.* (See Equipment, page 4.)

dry bread crumbs or graham cracker crumbs for the mold
4 ounces dried figs (6 to 10 figs)
½ cup milk
¼ cup (½ stick) unsalted butter plus butter for mold and wax paper
1 cup fresh, soft whole wheat bread crumbs★, loosely packed
4 eggs, graded large, separated

½ cup granulated sugar
⅓ cup blanched almonds, finely ground★ (measure before chopping or grinding)
1 teaspoon pure vanilla extract
pinch of salt
whipped cream or sour cream sauce (recipe follows)

Heavily butter the pudding mold, including the inside of the lid. Sprinkle the mold with bread crumbs or cracker crumbs and tap out the excess. Using the lid as a guide, cut out a round of wax paper that will just fit the top of the mold. Butter one side of the paper and set aside. You will need a stock pot or kettle large enough to enclose the mold and a metal rack or

★ These can be easily prepared in a *food processor*.

ring from a mason jar lid. Put a few inches of water to boil in the stock pot and put up a kettle to boil. (You will need to add boiling water to the pot when you put in the mold.)

Cut the figs into small pieces (about ½ inch) and remove and discard the stems. Place the figs in a small, heavy-bottomed saucepan with the milk and bring just to a boil over moderate heat. Simmer for 3 or 4 minutes and remove from the heat. Add the butter and stir until it is melted. Stir in the bread crumbs and set aside to cool.

In a large bowl beat the yolks with an electric mixer until they are very pale and thick. Gradually add the sugar while continuing to beat. With a rubber spatula fold in the cooled bread mixture, then the almonds and vanilla.

In a clean bowl with clean beaters, beat the egg whites until they are foamy. Add a tiny pinch of salt and continue to beat until the whites hold soft peaks. Gently fold them into the yolk mixture until no white is visible. Pour and scrape the batter into the prepared mold. Cover with the wax paper round, butter side down, and the lid. Put the rack or mason jar ring in the stock pot (use long tongs or a wooden spoon to position it in the center), set the mold on the ring, and pour in boiling water to reach two thirds of the way up the mold; return the water to a boil. Cover the stock pot and simmer on very low heat for 1 hour and 15 minutes. Remove the mold from the stock pot, wipe the lid, and carefully remove it and the paper. Allow the pudding to rest for 4 or 5 minutes before turning it out onto a plate. Serve at once with whipped cream or sour cream sauce (recipe follows).

Yield: 4 to 6 servings

Sour Cream Sauce

---

1 cup dairy sour cream
½ cup heavy cream
3 tablespoons confectioners' sugar

2 tablespoons lemon juice, freshly
    squeezed

Combine all ingredients and beat with a whisk until thoroughly combined and thick. Refrigerate, tightly covered, for at least 30 minutes before serving.

Yield: approximately 1¾ cups

The addition of a teaspoon of cream of tartar to the kettle of water will prevent a steamed-pudding mold from discoloring.

Tomato Summer Pudding

Summer pudding is a popular British dessert made by compressing fresh berries, bread, and sugar in a mold for several hours. Made instead with ripe, juicy tomatoes and fresh basil, it becomes a delightful summer teatime savory.

1½ tablespoons olive oil plus oil for the mold
1 clove garlic, split
2½ pounds very ripe tomatoes
¼ cup (loosely packed) fresh basil, chopped, plus leaves for garnish

½ teaspoon sugar
salt and pepper to taste
pinch of hot red pepper flakes
1 medium loaf French or Italian bread

Warm the oil and garlic in a skillet over low heat for 5 minutes to flavor the oil lightly. Discard the garlic and set aside the oil.

Core the tomatoes, cut them into quarters, and process them briefly in a *food processor* or chop them by hand in a bowl. Add and mix in the olive oil, basil, sugar, salt, pepper, and red pepper. Cut the bread into ⅓-inch slices.

Lightly grease a 6-cup bowl with a few drops of olive oil. Cover the bottom of the bowl with bread slices neatly trimmed to fit (they will become the top of the pudding). Spoon about a third of the tomato mixture over the bread. Cover most of the tomato layer with another layer of bread (don't bother trimming it), and alternate 2 more layers of tomatoes and 2 of bread, ending with bread. Depending on the size of the loaf, you may have bread left over.

Loosely cover the bowl with plastic wrap and place a flat plate on top of the plastic. (The plate should fit just inside the rim of the bowl.) Place a weight (a heavy tin of food or a rock will do) on the plate to compress the contents of the bowl and place it all on a plate with a lip to catch any tomato juice that may overflow. Refrigerate overnight.

Just before serving, unwrap the bowl and loosen the pudding by running a thin knife or spatula around the inside of the bowl. Unmold onto a serving plate and garnish with fresh basil leaves.

Yield: 6 to 8 wedges

Tomato teapot: Japan 1950s

♦ *(left) Sun-dried Tomato & Basil Sandwiches (page 62)*

♦ *(right) Tomato Summer Pudding (page 59)*

Sun-dried Tomato & Basil Sandwiches

Two-toned sandwiches are wonderfully decorative and couldn't be easier to make. Alternate the light- and dark-bread sides on your serving plate for the full effect. Warning: don't be tempted to make basil butter with dried basil; it really doesn't work. Use the freshest, greenest basil leaves available.

⅓ cup sun-dried tomatoes packed in oil
2 tablespoons walnuts
4 ounces cream cheese
2 tablespoons Parmesan cheese, preferably freshly grated
12 slices very *thinly sliced whole wheat bread* (Pepperidge Farm Very Thin is excellent)

12 slices very *thinly sliced white bread* (Pepperidge Farm Very Thin is excellent)
¾ cup basil butter (recipe follows)

Drain the oil from the tomatoes, leaving whatever oil clings to them, and cut into 1-inch pieces. Cut or break the walnuts into large pieces. Cut the cream cheese into small pieces. Add the tomatoes, grated Parmesan cheese, walnuts, and cream cheese to the work bowl of a *food processor* or blender and process until combined but not altogether smooth.

Working quickly (the bread becomes dry when exposed to the air), spread the mixture evenly over 1 side of each slice of whole wheat bread. Spread 1 side of each slice of white bread with basil butter (recipe follows) and place, butter side down, over the tomato-cheese mixture to make 12 sandwiches. To trim them, you can either use a sharp biscuit or cookie cutter for round sandwiches, *or* use a serrated knife to cut off the crusts on all sides and cut each sandwich into 3 finger-shaped pieces.

Arrange the sandwiches on a serving plate, alternating the light and dark sides up, cover them with paper towels that have been dipped into cold water and wrung out, then wrap the plate securely in plastic wrap or aluminum foil. Refrigerate up to several hours if desired. Bring to room temperature and uncover just before serving.

Yield: 12 to 36 tea sandwiches

Basil Butter

◆

½ cup (1 stick) unsalted butter
¼ teaspoon sugar
few drops of lemon juice, freshly
squeezed

½ cup chopped fresh basil leaves

Combine all ingredients in a *food processor* or blender and process until smooth. Spoon onto plastic wrap and shape into a log. Wrap securely and chill. This can be refrigerated for up to 3 days, or frozen for up to 1 month.

Yield: approximately ¾ cup

> It is easier to slice bread thinly if the loaf is cold. Use a serrated knife.

The Best Iced Tea

Generally believed to have been introduced at the 1904 World's Fair in St. Louis, iced tea has become one of the most popular beverages in the United States. (The Tea Council, a trade group, claims that more than 100 million Americans drink iced tea on any given day.) Currently, it can be bought in many ready-to-drink forms, but I will go out on a limb and state that none is as good-tasting, thirst-quenching, and generally delightful as cold-brewed, syrup-sweetened tea. The only disadvantage to preparing iced tea my way is the amount of time it takes to brew; you do have to plan ahead. The advantages, other than the obvious superior flavor, are: appearance—a *clear,* amber-colored liquid; no bitter taste—therefore, less sweetener, if any, is required; and a truer, less diluted tea flavor because only a little ice is needed. This method works for all types of tea: bags, loose leaves, decaffeinated, herbal—your choice. In the evening, mix up a batch (you won't even have to wait for the water to boil) and it'll be ready the following day. If you like a sweet drink, use homemade sugar syrup, which will not cloud the tea or settle on the bottom. Make a quantity of the simple syrup and use as needed. Refrigerated, it will keep indefinitely.

5 teabags or *5 teaspoons loose tea*
1 quart cold tap water or bottled water
1 tablespoon (or to taste) sugar syrup
    (recipe follows)

fruit slices, berries, or mint leaves for
    garnish (optional)

Measure the water into a glass pitcher or refrigerator bottle. If your tap water is poor quality, use bottled water instead. Knot the teabag strings together so that they will be easy to remove and place them in the cold water. If you are using loose tea, spoon it into the cold water. Add the syrup (op-

Penguin teapot:
Jenny Lind and
Allan Walter
Animals & Co.
Santa Fe, New
Mexico
1990

◆ **The Best Iced Tea**
   with Sugar Syrup

◆ *Ginger Tea Cakes*
   (page 67)

◆ *Gingerbread*
   (page 68)

tional) and stir once. Cover and refrigerate for at least 8 hours, preferably overnight.

Remove the teabags and discard. If you have used loose tea, strain the liquid first through a very fine sieve and again through a filter-paper-lined or muslin-lined sieve. Chill until ready to serve. Serve over ice and, if you like, garnish with fresh fruit slices, berries, or mint leaves, depending on the tea used and your preference.

Yield: 4 servings

Sugar Syrup for Iced Tea

◆

1 pound (about 2⅓ cups) superfine sugar
2¼ cups cold water

rind (zest) of 1 lemon in strips
(optional)

Combine all ingredients in a heavy-bottomed saucepan and slowly bring to a boil over medium-low heat, stirring occasionally. Simmer the mixture for 6 to 8 minutes. The syrup should be clear and, if you have used the lemon zest, will be light, amber-colored. Set aside to cool for about 15 minutes before removing the lemon zest and pouring into a glass jar with a tight-fitting lid. Cool completely in the jar, uncovered, before refrigerating.

Yield: about 2½ cups syrup

Iced tea originated in 1904 at the World's Fair in St. Louis when an Englishman, Richard Blechynden, had difficulty interesting people in the hot tea he was promoting because the weather was so warm. In desperation, he offered it served over ice. Today about 80 percent of all the tea consumed in the United States is iced; according to the Tea Council, a trade group, more than half the U.S. population drinks tea on any given day.

Ginger Tea Cakes

◆

Soft, cakelike cookies are traditionally known as tea cakes, and I always thought it was because their texture and flavor are enhanced by hot tea. Well, I've discovered that iced tea is just as good an accompaniment for these individual gingerbreads. Try them plain or spread with a bit of black currant jam.

2¼ cups unsifted all-purpose flour
1½ teaspoons baking soda
1 teaspoon unsweetened cocoa powder
½ teaspoon ground ginger
pinch of ground cinnamon
pinch of ground cloves
pinch of dry mustard
pinch of salt

½ cup (1 stick) unsalted butter, softened
½ cup granulated sugar
½ cup (scant) light molasses
1 egg, graded large
⅓ cup buttermilk, at room temperature
½ cup soft currants
black currant jam (optional)

Adjust 2 racks to divide the oven into thirds and preheat the oven to 350 degrees. Line cookie sheets with baking parchment or aluminum foil, shiny side up.

Sift the flour, soda, cocoa, ginger, cinnamon, cloves, dry mustard, and salt together and set aside.

Cream the butter and sugar until fluffy. Add the molasses and beat until smooth. Add the egg and beat well. Add the sifted dry ingredients in 3 parts, alternating with the buttermilk in 2 parts, mixing only until smooth after each addition. Stir in the currants.

Using a measuring spoon and a tiny rubber spatula, drop the dough by rounded tablespoonfuls 2½ to 3 inches apart (they spread) onto the lined cookie sheets. Try to keep the cookies round and uniform in size.

Bake 2 sheets at a time for 14 to 16 minutes or until the cookies are brown all over and the tops spring back sharply when pressed gently. Reverse the sheets top to bottom and back to front after 8 minutes to ensure even baking. Slide the parchment or foil onto a flat surface and allow the cookies to cool for about 3 minutes before transferring them with a metal spatula to a wire rack to cool completely. Serve plain or with black currant jam. Store in an airtight container (without the jam) with wax paper between the layers for up to 3 days.

Yield: 2½ dozen tea cakes

Black currant tea makes particularly good iced tea (see page 65) and is lovely served with black currant jam and scones (see page 25) or Cream Cheese and Jelly Muffins (see page 108) made with black currant jam.

Gingerbread

For me, gingerbread is the perfect teatime food: not too sweet, not too spicy, not too plain, not too fancy. It is wonderful served warm in cold weather or at room temperature anytime. And, although I used to think of it as a "winter treat," it is especially refreshing with iced tea on a hot day. If you're having guests for tea, bake gingerbread right before they're expected; the divine aroma from your kitchen will let everyone know it's homemade.

1 cup unsifted all-purpose flour
½ cup unsifted whole wheat flour
1 teaspoon baking powder
½ teaspoon baking soda
1½ teaspoons ground ginger
pinch of black pepper, freshly ground★
pinch of cinnamon★
pinch of cloves★

pinch of dry mustard★
pinch of salt
½ cup (1 stick) unsalted butter, softened
½ cup granulated sugar
½ cup light molasses
½ cup dairy sour cream
2 eggs, graded large

Position an oven rack in the center of the oven and preheat the oven to 350 degrees. Grease an 8-inch square pan with butter or no-stick cooking spray. Dust lightly with flour and tap out excess. Set aside.

In a medium bowl stir and toss the flours, baking powder, baking soda, spices, and salt together with a wire whisk or fork until evenly distributed. Set aside.

In a large bowl with an electric mixer or by hand with a wooden spoon, cream the butter and sugar until light and fluffy. Add the molasses and sour cream and mix thoroughly. Add the eggs and beat until combined. The mixture will look curdled; it's to be expected. Add the dry ingredients and stir until incorporated and smooth. Pour the batter into the prepared pan and bake in the center of the oven for 35 to 40 minutes or until the gingerbread is lightly browned all over, the middle barely comes back when pressed gently with your finger, and, most important, a wooden toothpick inserted in the middle comes out clean, with no uncooked batter on it.

★ Add spices to taste. A pinch of each is enough for me. Hint: children prefer mildly spiced gingerbread.

Allow the cake to rest in the pan on a rack for 5 minutes. Run a knife between the cake and pan to loosen the cake and turn it out onto a rack to cool.

Yield: 8 portions, 2 inches by 4 inches

———

Crunchy Wheat Cookies

◆

There was an old woman
Who lived in a shoe.
She had so many children
She didn't know what to do.

I know what she could have done at teatime to keep her brood happy—serve a batch of these. Not only are they delicious, but the crunchy texture and high fiber content of these big cookies make them very satisfying to young appetites.

Old Woman in the Shoe teapot: Lingard Pottery England 1930s

◆ *(left) Prune-Apricot Bars (page 73)*

◆ *(right) Crunchy Wheat Cookies*

1 cup Wheatena cereal, uncooked
¾ cup unsifted all-purpose flour
¼ cup unsifted whole wheat flour
½ teaspoon baking soda
½ teaspoon baking powder
pinch of salt
½ cup shredded coconut, sweetened or unsweetened
⅔ cup soft raisins

½ cup chopped walnuts (optional)
½ cup unsalted butter (1 stick), softened
½ cup turbinado sugar (Sugar in the Raw) or ½ cup granulated sugar
½ cup dark brown sugar, firmly packed
1 egg, graded large
¼ teaspoon pure vanilla extract
few drops pure almond extract

Position 2 oven racks to divide the oven into thirds and preheat the oven to 375 degrees. Line cookie sheets with baking parchment or aluminum foil, shiny side up, and set aside.

In a small bowl whisk together the cereal, flours, baking soda, baking powder, and salt and set aside.

In another small bowl toss the coconut, raisins, and walnuts with a heaping teaspoon of the reserved dry ingredients until evenly distributed. Set aside.

Cream the butter with the sugars until fluffy. Add the egg, vanilla extract, and almond extract and beat until combined. Gradually add the dry ingredients and mix until just incorporated. Stir in the coconut, raisins, and walnuts.

Measure a scant ¼ cup of dough in a ¼-cup dry measure and roll the dough in your hands into a ball. Place 5 balls on each cookie sheet (these will spread). Use the flat bottom of a drinking glass (dipped into cold water to keep it from sticking to the dough) to press each ball into a 3-inch cookie, ⅓ to ½ inch high. Bake the cookies, 2 sheets at a time, for 11 to 15 minutes or until they are lightly browned all over, darker at the edges, and the center barely springs back when gently pressed with your fingertip. Rotate the sheets top to bottom and front to back after 7 minutes to ensure even baking. Allow the cookies to rest on the sheets for a minute or two before carefully transferring them with a large metal spatula to a wire rack to cool completely. Store in an airtight container.

Yield: 15 4-inch cookies

Give the kids a hot-weather teatime treat of frozen cookies. Serve them right from the freezer; the cookies will "sweat" if left to come to room temperature after they are unwrapped.

Prune-Apricot Bars

◆

Stewed fruits are not just for old ladies. The sweet/tart puree, sandwiched between rich, crunchy pastry, should delight anyone, regardless of age.

½ cup dried apricots, cut into raisin-size pieces
½ cup pitted prunes, cut into raisin-size pieces
¼ cup lemon juice, freshly squeezed
¼ cup water
1 teaspoon grated lemon rind (zest)
1 cup plus 2 tablespoons old-fashioned rolled oats

½ cup (1 stick) unsalted butter, softened
¼ cup light brown sugar, firmly packed
¼ cup granulated sugar
½ cup plus 2 tablespoons unsifted all-purpose flour
¼ teaspoon ground cinnamon
pinch of salt

Position an oven rack in the center of the oven and preheat the oven to 375 degrees. Line an 8-inch-by-8-inch pan with aluminum foil: cut a piece of foil 12 inches square, then mold it evenly, shiny side down, over the outside bottom of the pan. Remove the foil and place it in the pan, shiny side up. With a pot holder, smooth the corners against the pan (without the pot holder the foil is likely to tear). Lightly but thoroughly grease the foil with melted butter or no-stick cooking spray. Set aside.

Combine the apricots, prunes, lemon juice, water, and lemon zest in a heavy-bottomed saucepan. Over moderate heat bring to a boil, stirring and mashing the mixture. Simmer for 6 minutes, all the while stirring and mashing. The mixture will be thick. Remove it from the heat and allow to cool.

Place the oats in a baking pan that has sides at least 1 inch high and bake in the preheated oven for 10 minutes. Stir with a wooden spoon every 3 minutes or so to ensure even toasting. Set aside to cool.

In a large bowl cream the butter with the sugars until fluffy. Sift the flour, cinnamon, and salt together and stir into the butter-sugar mixture. Stir in the cooled oats. Spoon half the dough into the foil-lined pan and spread it evenly with the back of a spoon or a spatula. The dough is sticky, so it will take a bit of time and patience to spread it. Smooth the cooled apricot-prune puree over the dough in the pan. Scrape the remaining dough onto a large piece of wax paper, place a second piece of wax paper over it, and, with a rolling pin, roll out a 7½-inch square. Use the bottom of the prepared pan as a guide. Lift off the top piece of wax paper and cut and patch the dough to make an even square. Slide the dough, with the wax paper underneath it, onto a cookie sheet or board and place it all in the freezer for about 5 minutes until the dough is stiff. Remove it from the freezer, invert the dough over the prepared pan, peel off the wax paper, and gently press the stiff dough onto the puree.

Bake in the middle of the oven for 40 to 50 minutes until the cake is lightly browned all over, perhaps a bit darker at the edges. Cool the cake in the pan on a rack. When cool to the touch, invert the cake onto a board and remove the pan. Gently peel off the foil and discard. Invert the cake onto a cutting board. Cut into bars. As with most bars, these will have neater edges if chilled for an hour before cutting.

Yield: 12 bars, approximately 1½ inches by 4 inches, or 16 squares, 2 inches by 2 inches

---

Before precutting bars or cakes, consider the size of the tea plates you will be using and portion accordingly. Chilled cakes will slice more easily and cleanly; use a ruler to achieve even squares or rectangles.

Welsh Rabbit Rounds

◆

At some point in our culinary development it was considered amusing to give grand names to ordinary foods and beverages. For example, Adam's Ale for water, Cape Cod Turkey for codfish, and Welsh Rabbit for melted cheese on toast (Welsh Rarebit is an even grander name for the same dish). I've adapted the traditional soupy rabbit to one more suitable for teatime. These open-faced sandwiches are easy to make and easy to eat.

18 slices very fresh, very thin whole
    wheat bread (Pepperidge Farm
    Very Thin is just right)
½ pound (2 cups) sharp Cheddar cheese,
    grated
1 tablespoon dry, unflavored bread
    crumbs

1 tablespoon light or heavy cream
1 teaspoon Worcestershire sauce
pinch of cayenne pepper
pinch of dry mustard
2 to 3 tablespoons ale or beer
paprika for garnish

Preheat the oven to 400 degrees. Butter the cups of a tartlet pan with very shallow cups: ¼ inch deep and 2½ inches across. (You can use a muffin pan if that is all that is available, but the result will be more like rabbit cups than rabbit sandwiches.)

Using a 3-inch cookie or biscuit cutter, cut a round from each slice of bread. Press each round into a tartlet cup so that the bread is flattened all over. Bake the bread rounds, or croustades, for 10 to 15 minutes until they are crisp and golden. Remove them from the tartlet pans and place them on a wire rack to cool slightly.

While the croustades are baking, prepare the cheese mixture. In a medium bowl combine the cheese, bread crumbs, cream, Worcestershire sauce,

cayenne pepper, and dry mustard. Gradually add the ale or beer until the mixture forms a stiff paste.

Lower the oven temperature to 350 degrees. Spread the cheese mixture on the croustades, leaving a ¼-inch margin all around. Mound the cheese higher in the middle. Place the rounds on a baking sheet and bake for 10 minutes or until the cheese is melted throughout and beginning to brown. Do not let the edges of the croustades burn. Remove from the oven, sprinkle with paprika, and serve warm.

Yield: 18 small open-faced sandwiches

> Tea left to steep more than 5 minutes will be bitter. Either make just enough for a single cup each *or* strain the tea, as soon as it is ready, into a second, heated teapot.

Bunny Bites
(Miniature Carrot Muffins)

Mixed quickly and easily in a saucepan, these tiny, sweet carrot muffins contain only a small amount of shortening and no eggs. Easy, quick, relatively healthy, *and* delicious—a perfect teatime recipe. You'll need miniature muffin cups measuring approximately 1¾ inches across and ½ inch deep.

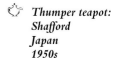

Thumper teapot:
Shafford
Japan
1950s

◆ *(left) **Bunny Bites***

◆ *(right) **Welsh Rabbit Rounds** (page 75)*

◆◆

⅓ cup granulated sugar
⅓ cup water
1 tablespoon unsalted butter
¼ cup coarsely grated carrot (1 large
    carrot)
¼ cup currants or chopped raisins
½ teaspoon ground cinnamon
pinch of nutmeg, preferably freshly ground

pinch of salt
½ cup unsifted all-purpose flour
¼ teaspoon baking powder
¼ teaspoon baking soda
½ cup (scant) walnuts, chopped into
    currant-size pieces

Stir the sugar, water, butter, grated carrot, currants (or chopped raisins), cinnamon, nutmeg, and salt together in a medium, heavy-bottomed saucepan and bring to a boil over medium-high heat. Boil for 4 minutes, stirring often. Remove the saucepan from the heat and allow the mixture to cool to lukewarm, at least 30 minutes.

Position 2 oven racks to divide the oven into thirds and preheat the oven to 350 degrees. Grease or spray with no-stick cooking spray 18 miniature muffin cups (most muffin trays have 12 cups). Set aside.

In a small bowl whisk the baking powder and baking soda into the flour until they are evenly distributed. Add these dry ingredients to the cooled carrot mixture in the saucepan and fold gently with a wooden spoon or spatula 1 or 2 times. Add the walnuts and continue to fold only until the flour is no longer visible. Spoon the batter into the greased muffin cups, just filling each cup (level, not rounded). If there is not enough batter to fill all the cups in your pan, spoon a teaspoon of water into each of the empty cups. This will prevent the pans from burning and will add moisture to the muffins.

Place the pans next to each other, if there is room, on the upper oven rack, or place one pan on each of 2 racks, positioned so that one is not directly

◆◆

over the other. Bake for about 12 to 15 minutes or until the muffins are firm to the touch and a wooden toothpick inserted in the center of a muffin comes out clean. Allow the muffins to rest in the pans for 4 to 5 minutes before turning them out onto a rack to cool. They can be served warm or at room temperature. Leftover muffins can be frozen in self-sealing plastic bags for up to 1 month. To reheat them, place them, frozen, on cookie sheets and bake in a preheated 350-degree oven for 10 minutes.

Yield: 18 tiny muffins

An excellent carrier for muffins-to-go is the tin in which they were baked.

Chocolate Jumbles
(Chocolate-Cherry Jumble Holes)

Ring-shaped English biscuits—or cookies—are called jumbles. Supposedly the name comes from "gimbal" or "gemel," meaning a finger ring shaped from two separate loops. The original recipe was said to be found at the site of the Battle of Bosworth Field (1485), where Richard III's cook dropped it during the last battle of the Wars of the Roses. Recipes for jumbles have evolved over the years from plain to fancy. Here's one of the best ways to make jumbles.

3 ounces (3 squares) unsweetened
    chocolate
7 tablespoons (1 stick less 1 tablespoon)
    unsalted butter, softened
1 cup granulated sugar plus additional
    for decoration
1 egg, graded large
1 teaspoon instant-espresso or -coffee
    powder dissolved in 1 tablespoon
    hot water

2 cups less 1 tablespoon all-purpose flour
    (sift before measuring)
1 tablespoon unsweetened cocoa powder,
    preferably Dutch-processed
1½ teaspoons baking powder
½ teaspoon baking soda
pinch of salt

Melt the chocolate squares in a double boiler over hot, not boiling, water or in a microwave oven until it is mostly—but not all—melted. Remove from the heat and stir until all the chocolate melts and it is smooth. Set it aside to cool slightly.

Using an electric mixer or a wooden spoon, cream the butter and 1 cup of sugar in a large bowl until fluffy. Add the egg and the dissolved instant coffee and beat until combined. Mix in the cooled chocolate. Stir the cocoa powder, baking powder, baking soda, and salt into the flour and add to the dough, mixing until the dry ingredients are absorbed. Scrape the dough, which will be sticky, onto a large sheet of wax paper or plastic wrap, shape it into 2 equal flat, round disks, then wrap and refrigerate them for at least 1 hour and at most overnight.

When you are ready to bake, position an oven rack in the center of the oven and preheat the oven to 350 degrees. Line cookie sheets with baking parchment or aluminum foil, shiny side up. Set aside.

Working with 1 portion of dough at a time, place it between 2 12-inch squares of wax paper and roll it with a rolling pin to a thickness of ¼ inch. Lift and replace the top and bottom wax paper as often as necessary to

Red Doughnut teapot: Hall China Company East Liverpool, Ohio 1930s

◆ *(left) Chocolate-Cherry Jumble Holes (page 82)*

◆ *(center) Lemon Rings with Lemon Curd (page 83)*

◆ *(right) Chocolate Jumbles (page 79)*

smooth any wrinkles that result from rolling. Slide the dough, still between the wax paper, onto a cutting board or cookie sheet and place it in the freezer for 5 to 10 minutes while you roll out the rest of the dough. Remove the chilled and somewhat stiff dough from the freezer and lift off the top paper. Using a doughnut cutter dipped in whole wheat flour or cocoa powder to keep it from sticking, cut out as many rounds as possible. Using a small metal spatula, carefully transfer the rings to the prepared cookie sheet. Place the rings about 1½ inches apart. You can either reroll the center rounds of dough or bake them along with the rings and make jumble holes (recipe follows). If you want to bake them, place them 1 inch apart in the center of the cookie sheet, where it will be less hot; place the rings toward the outside. Sprinkle the rings with granulated sugar; do not add sugar to the holes. Bake 1 sheet at a time (chocolate cookies burn easily and should be watched carefully while baking) for 11 to 13 minutes until the cookies feel firm to the touch and just spring back when gently pressed with your fingertip. Slide the parchment or foil onto a flat surface and let the cookies rest for a minute or two before transferring them with a metal spatula to a rack to cool completely. Reroll the scraps of dough and repeat. Store the jumbles airtight for up to 1 week.

Yield: 22 to 24 3-inch cookies

Chocolate-Cherry Jumble Holes

◆

I have noticed that, given a choice, children will choose big cookies and adults will choose small ones. Serve the jumble holes and jumbles at a family tea and watch what happens.

22 to 24 1-inch rounds from Chocolate
    Jumbles, baked and cooled
Morello cherry preserves (the best quality
    available)

confectioners' sugar for decoration

Shortly before serving these cookies, spread the bottom (flat side) of half the rounds with a small amount of preserves. Do not spread it all the way to the edges of the cookie. Cover the preserves with the flat side of the remaining cookies. Put a tablespoon or so of confectioners' sugar in a fine sieve and sprinkle it lightly over the tops of the sandwiches.

Yield: 11 to 12 small sandwich cookies

Lemon Rings

◆

Rich butter cookies spread with homemade lemon curd can change a run-of-the-mill tea break into an elegant affair. A recipe for Raspberry Rings in my earlier cookbook, *The Cookie Jar Cookbook,* is similar and has been so popular that I am including this version.

¾ cup (1½ sticks) unsalted butter
1½ cups unsifted all-purpose flour
⅓ cup granulated sugar

confectioners' sugar for decoration
½ cup (approximately) lemon curd
    spread (recipe follows)

To prepare the dough in a *food processor* (and I recommend this method), the butter must be very cold. Using a heavy knife, cut it into ½-inch cubes. Measure the flour into the work bowl of the processor and add the cold cubes of butter. Pulse the machine on and off until the mixture looks like coarse meal. Add the granulated sugar and process until all the ingredients are blended. The mixture will not form a ball, so do not overprocess waiting for this to happen. Turn it out into a large bowl or onto a large sheet of wax paper and knead briefly until the dough holds together and is smooth. Divide it into 2 equal portions, wrap them securely in wax paper or plastic wrap, and refrigerate for at least 1 hour.

To prepare the dough *without a food processor,* stir the flour and granulated sugar together in a large bowl. Cut the softened butter cubes into the dry ingredients with a pastry blender or 2 table knives until the mixture resembles coarse meal or fresh, soft bread crumbs. Knead briefly until the dough holds together and is smooth. Continue as above.

When you are ready to bake, position an oven rack in the middle of the oven and preheat the oven to 325 degrees. Line cookie sheets with baking parchment or aluminum foil, shiny side up. Set aside.

Work with 1 portion of dough at a time, keeping the other refrigerated. With a rolling pin, roll the dough between large pieces of wax paper to a thickness of ¼ inch. Lift and replace the top and bottom sheets of wax paper as often as necessary to smooth any wrinkles that result from rolling. Slide the dough, still between the wax paper, onto a cookie sheet and place in the refrigerator for about 15 minutes until the dough is cool and slightly stiff. Roll and chill the second portion of dough the same way.

Remove the first portion of dough from the refrigerator, lift off the top sheet of wax paper, and replace it gently. Turn over the "package" of dough and remove the wax paper now on top. Using a floured round cookie cutter, quickly cut out as many cookies as possible. Transfer them with a metal spatula to the lined cookie sheets, placing them 1½ inches apart. If they have become too soft to transfer easily, slide the wax paper onto a cookie sheet or board and place in the freezer for a few minutes until the rounds are firm. Using a smaller floured round cutter (or a thimble), cut out the centers of half the cookies on the sheets to make rings. Press all the scraps together, wrap them, and refrigerate.

Bake the rounds and rings 1 sheet at a time in the center of the oven for 13 to 16 minutes or until they are a pale golden-brown, a bit darker at the edges. Rotate the sheets front to back after 8 minutes to ensure even baking. Allow the cookies to rest for a minute or so before transferring them with a metal spatula to wire racks to cool completely. Cut out and bake the remaining dough and scraps in the same way.

Shortly before serving, sift confectioners' sugar over the rings. Spread the flat side of each round with lemon curd (or thick fruit preserves, if you prefer). Place a ring, sugared side up, over each round and fill the center with a bit more filling. Store the cookies (without the lemon curd) in an airtight tin for up to 3 days or in the freezer for up to 1 month. Once filled with lemon curd, the cookies can be stored in the refrigerator for up to 3 days.

Yield: approximately 1 dozen 2½-inch sandwich cookies

As a rule, rolled cookies will not spread as much as dropped cookies and can be placed closer together on the baking sheet.

Lemon Curd

◆

1 egg, graded large
1 egg yolk, graded large
1⅓ cups confectioners' sugar
⅓ cup lemon juice, freshly squeezed and
    strained
2 teaspoons grated lemon rind (zest)

3 tablespoons unsalted butter, softened
    and cut into bits
For curd to be baked in tarts: 1 fully
    baked 8-inch pastry shell or 4 to 8
    individual shells

In the top of a double boiler or in a glass bowl set over a saucepan of simmering water, place the egg, egg yolk, sugar, lemon juice, and lemon zest. Cook the mixture, stirring, for 10 to 15 minutes or until it thickens enough to coat the back of a spoon. Remove from the heat and whisk in the butter, 1 small piece at a time, making sure that each piece is melted before adding another.

Spoon into baked pastry shell[s] set on a baking sheet and bake in a preheated 375-degree oven for 6 to 10 minutes or until the curd bubbles up and puffs slightly. Cool before serving.

For curd to be used as a spread:
Follow instructions above until the mixture is thick enough to coat the back of a spoon. At that point, with the mixture still over the hot water, begin to add the bits of butter gradually, taking about 5 minutes to add it all, stirring continually. The mixture should be very hot, glossy, translucent, and the consistency of thin pudding. Remove it from the heat and pour and scrape it into 1 medium or 2 small jars with tight-fitting lids. Cool to room temperature uncovered. The curd can be refrigerated for up to 1 month.

Yield: about 1 cup

Granny Ann's Banana Bran Muffins

———◆———

The sprinkling of a tiny amount of cinnamon-sugar on these muffins makes them a favorite of the grandchildren in our family. The grandparents—and everyone else—like them for their good taste and good texture.

1 cup ready-to-eat wheat bran cereal
2 tablespoons apple juice
2 tablespoons milk
3 tablespoons butter, melted and cooled, or vegetable oil
1 cup mashed ripe banana (about 2 large bananas)
⅓ cup granulated or turbinado sugar (Sugar in the Raw)

1 cup all-purpose flour (sift before measuring)
½ cup unsifted whole wheat flour
2 teaspoons baking powder
½ teaspoon baking soda
1 egg, graded large
1 tablespoon granulated sugar plus a pinch of ground cinnamon (optional)

Position an oven rack in the center of the oven and preheat the oven to 375 degrees. Grease muffin cups with butter or no-stick cooking spray or line them with paper baking cups. Set aside.

In a medium bowl combine the bran cereal, apple juice, milk, butter or oil, banana, and sugar. Set aside for a few minutes to allow the cereal to soften.

In a medium bowl whisk together the white flour, whole wheat flour, baking powder, and baking soda. Set aside.

Add the egg to the cereal mixture and beat to combine. The mixture will be lumpy because of the banana. Add the dry ingredients all at once and gently fold only until the dry ingredients are no longer visible. Do not overmix. Spoon about ¼ cup of the batter into each of the prepared muffin cups (fill-

ing them no more than ⅔ full). Sprinkle the tops with about ¼ teaspoon of the cinnamon-sugar mixture (if using). Bake in the center of the oven for about 25 minutes until a wooden toothpick inserted in the center of a muffin comes out clean, with no unbaked batter on it. Allow the muffins to cool in the pans for 4 or 5 minutes before turning them out onto a wire rack to cool further. They can be served warm or at room temperature. Like most muffins, they freeze well. To reheat, place frozen muffins on a baking sheet in a 350-degree preheated oven for 10 to 15 minutes.

Yield: 12 2½-inch muffins

To be sure overripe bananas will be available when you are ready to bake, keep a supply in your freezer. Ripen bananas at room temperature until the skins are spotted with black, remove the skins, wrap the fruit individually in plastic wrap and aluminum foil, and freeze. To use, unwrap and place on a plate until they are soft enough to mash with a fork. If the bananas give off liquid while defrosting, be sure to use it in the recipe.

Ginger Shortbread

◆

While this is a recipe definitely not devised by my granny (she never knew the wonders of the food processor), the resulting cookie is old-fashioned in its texture, simplicity, and delicious taste; a natural with tea. If a food processor is unavailable, simply cream the softened butter with the sugar and

Granny Ann teapot: Shawnee Pottery Zanesville, Ohio 1950s

◆ *(left) Ginger Shortbread Wedges and Rounds*

◆ *(right) Granny Ann's Banana Bran Muffins (page 87)*

lemon zest, stir in the preserves, then the flour and ground ginger; chill the dough until it is firm enough to roll out and proceed with the recipe as written below. If you prefer an alternative to rolling and cutting the dough, see the NOTE on page 91.

1 cup unsifted all-purpose flour
3 tablespoons sifted confectioners' sugar
¼ teaspoon ground ginger

¼ teaspoon grated lemon rind (zest)
½ cup (1 stick) unsalted butter, very cold
2 tablespoons ginger preserves, chilled

Position an oven rack in the center of the oven and preheat the oven to 300 degrees. Line a cookie sheet with parchment paper or use it *un*greased.

Put the flour, sugar, ginger, and lemon zest into the work bowl of a *food processor* and, with the steel blade in place, pulse the machine 3 or 4 times to mix the dry ingredients. Cut the cold butter into at least 8 pieces and add them to the work bowl. Pulse until the mixture looks like coarse meal. Add the preserves and run the machine until the dough just comes together into a ball. Do not overprocess. Turn the dough out onto a large sheet of wax paper, flatten it slightly, cover it with another sheet of wax paper, and, with a rolling pin, roll it evenly to about ⅜ inch thick. Lift and replace the top and bottom sheets of wax paper as often as necessary to smooth any wrinkles that result from rolling. Slide the dough, still between the wax paper, onto a cookie sheet and place it in the freezer for 5 or 10 minutes until it is firm.

Remove the top sheet of wax paper and, using a *floured* 2-inch round cookie cutter, cut out as many rounds as possible. If the dough feels too soft to lift the rounds onto the cookie sheet easily, slide the wax paper with the rounds on it onto a cookie sheet or board and put it back in the freezer for a few minutes.

Reroll the scraps of dough and cut out as above. Place the rounds about 1 inch apart on the lined or ungreased cookie sheet (the shortbread will spread very little). Using a toothpick or fork, prick 2 or 3 holes in the top of each round. Bake for 30 to 35 minutes until the center of the cookies are firm and the edges are lightly browned. Rotate the sheet front to back after 20 minutes to ensure even baking. Allow the cookies to rest for 2 or 3 minutes before transferring them with a metal spatula to a wire rack to cool completely. Store these airtight for 2 or 3 days.

Yield: 16 2-inch cookies

NOTE: If you want to bake shortbread more quickly, after turning the dough out of the food processor, cut it into 2 even pieces. Put them on the lined or ungreased cookie sheet and, with your fingers, pat them into 2 even rounds, about 5 inches across and ⅜ inch thick. Leave as much room as possible between the 2 cakes. With a *floured* fork, make a decorative edge around the cakes by pressing the tines lightly into the dough; prick the dough uniformly in a few places on top of the rounds. Bake as above. When done, allow the cakes to rest for 2 or 3 minutes, then, using a long, sharp knife, cut each one into 8 wedges (like a pie) by pressing the knife through the dough; don't use a sawing motion. Wait 2 or 3 minutes more before transferring the wedges to a rack to cool thoroughly.

Buy spices in small quantities, as they often lose their effectiveness after one year. Mark the date you open the jar or tin on the label and replace it a year later or when it has lost its pungent fragrance.

Cat's Tongues
(Langues de Chat)

◆

I remember these cookies as my favorites in the butter-cookie assortment my mother used to buy at a fancy French bakery. I'm not sure if, as a child, I was attracted to the cookies or their fanciful name. Now I know it's the taste and texture of the paper-thin, buttery slivers that I adore. The following recipe makes about 50, which is actually a small batch. At one delicate mouthful each, they are sure to disappear quickly. I recommend storing them in the freezer (they defrost quickly) to maintain their crispness.

½ cup all-purpose flour (sifted before measuring)
pinch of salt
6 tablespoons (¾ stick) unsalted butter, softened, plus additional butter for cookie sheets

⅓ cup superfine sugar
1 teaspoon grated lemon rind (zest)
2 egg whites, graded large

Position 2 oven racks to divide the oven into thirds and preheat the oven to 400 degrees. Grease 2 cookie sheets heavily with unsalted butter. The cookies won't spread evenly and may stick to the pans if they aren't thoroughly greased. And do use butter; it makes a difference in the rich flavor of the cookies. Set aside.

Either fit a 12- to 15-inch pastry bag with a plain ¼-inch round tip *or* cut a ¼-inch opening (tiny) at one of the bottom corners of a self-sealing plastic storage bag. Set aside.

Sift the flour and salt together twice and set aside.

In a medium bowl with an electric mixer or by hand with a wooden spoon, cream the butter, sugar, and lemon zest until fluffy. Add the egg whites and stir to incorporate. Sift the flour and salt over the batter and stir gently just until the dry ingredients are blended.

Spoon the batter into the prepared pastry bag or plastic bag. Twist the top of the bag to compress the batter and keep it from oozing out of the top, and carefully pipe 3-inch-long pencil-thin strips 2 inches apart (they spread) onto the prepared cookie sheets. Keep the strips thin and as even as possible so that they will spread and bake evenly.

Bake 2 sheets at a time for 5 to 7 minutes or until the cookies are flat and golden brown at the edges, but still pale in the center. Rotate the sheets top to bottom and front to back after 4 minutes to ensure even baking. As soon as the cookies are firm enough to remove from the sheets (30 seconds, usually), do so with a thin metal spatula. Place them on racks to cool completely. Be sure to cool, wipe clean, then rebutter the cookie sheets before baking the remaining batter.

Unless the "tongues" are going to be served immediately, place them, when cool, in a plastic freezer box with wax paper beween the layers, seal the box airtight, and keep frozen for up to 1 month. Defrost *in the airtight box* or the cookies will sweat and become soggy.

Yield: 50 very thin cookies

A baby-bottle nipple brush is perfect for cleaning pastry-tube tips and the inside of teapot spouts.

Molded Spice Cookies

◆

Cookies made in ceramic molds are charming to look at and, in this case, good to eat. In order for the dough to release from the mold and keep its shape, it has to be rather stiff and contain a minimum of leavening. The result is a thick, crisp cookie that is especially good with hot tea. Molding the cookies takes some patience but is not difficult.

1 cup plus 2 tablespoons granulated sugar
¼ cup plus 2 tablespoons water
3 tablespoons dark corn syrup
½ cup (1 stick) plus 1 tablespoon unsalted butter
vegetable oil for oiling the mold

3½ cups unsifted all-purpose flour
2 teaspoons ground cinnamon
1 teaspoon ground ginger
¼ teaspoon ground cloves
pinch of freshly ground black pepper (optional)
⅛ teaspoon baking soda

In a medium, heavy-bottomed saucepan combine the sugar, water, and corn syrup. Bring just to a boil over moderate heat, stirring often to dissolve the sugar. Remove from the heat and add the butter. When the butter is mostly melted, stir to combine and continue stirring until the butter is completely melted. Turn this into a large bowl and set aside to cool.

Position an oven rack in the center of the oven and preheat the oven to 350 degrees. Line a cookie sheet with parchment paper or aluminum foil, shiny side up. Set aside.

Lightly but thoroughly oil a ceramic cookie mold. I find the easiest way to do this is to pour a few drops of oil on the mold and spread it into every nook and cranny with my finger. If you have used more oil than just enough to coat the surface of the mold, blot the excess with a paper towel. Set aside.

Sift together the flour, cinnamon, ginger, cloves, and black pepper (if you are using it) and set aside. Dissolve the baking soda in 1 teaspoonful of warm tap water and add it to the cooled sugar-butter mixture. Gradually stir in the dry ingredients. The dough will become fairly stiff, so you may want to use your hand to mix in the last of the flour and spices.

Pinch off a piece of dough large enough to cover your mold and flatten it in your hand or on a piece of wax paper on a flat surface to the approximate shape of your mold. Place the flattened dough on the oiled surface of the mold and, with your fingertips, push the dough evenly into the mold. Either with a rolling pin or with the heel of your hand, press the dough firmly over the mold to get a good impression. Place the dough-filled mold in the freezer for 2 to 5 minutes until the dough is firm and will separate from the mold more readily. Now, with the point of a table knife or your finger, gently push an edge of the dough away from the edge of the mold to loosen it. If necessary, keep doing this along an edge until the dough separates from the mold. Turn the mold over and allow the dough to slip onto the prepared cookie sheet. With the point of a sharp knife, cut away any excess dough. Continue molding cookies with the remainder of the dough, lightly oiling the mold before each use. (You'll need less oil each time.) If you have only one mold and have to wait while the dough chills each time it is filled, keep the cookie sheet in the refrigerator so that the cookies won't lose their shape. The cookies won't spread much during baking, so place them 1 to 2 inches apart on the sheet.

Bake 1 sheet at a time for 12 to 15 minutes until the cookies are lightly browned at the edges. Rotate the sheet front to back after 7 minutes to ensure even baking. Allow the cookies to rest on the parchment or foil for 4 to

5 minutes before transferring them with a metal spatula to a wire rack to cool completely. They will become crisp when cool. Store in an airtight container for up to 1 week.

Yield: 10 6-inch-by-3-inch cookies

One cup of strong tea has from 25 percent to 60 percent of the caffeine in a cup of coffee.

Brownstone Peanut Cake

Single-family houses built in the first part of this century in New York City are referred to as brownstones. It doesn't take much imagination to understand the name; even if the stone wasn't originally brown, urban grime has made it so. But it is a mystery to me why certain cakes are called brownstone; there doesn't seem to be any single characteristic they share. Some are chocolate, some caramel, some round, some rectangular, and none have stones. Here is my offering in the brownstone category: a sweet, brown sugar cake with a candylike peanut topping. Baked in a ring mold, it is unusual-looking and uncommonly delicious.

Topping:
¼ cup (½ stick) unsalted butter
2 tablespoons dark corn syrup
1 tablespoon granulated sugar
1 tablespoon brown sugar (light or dark),
    firmly packed
1 tablespoon heavy cream
½ cup unsalted peanuts, coarsely chopped

Batter:
1¼ cups unsifted cake flour
1½ teaspoons baking powder
pinch of salt
¼ cup (½ stick) unsalted butter, softened
¾ cup brown sugar (light or dark), firmly
    packed
1 egg, graded large
½ teaspoon pure vanilla extract
½ cup buttermilk, at room temperature
2 tablespoons light molasses
½ teaspoon baking soda

Position an oven rack in the center of the oven and preheat the oven to 350 degrees. Thoroughly grease a 5-cup ring mold (even if it has a no-stick surface) with butter or no-stick cooking spray and set aside.

To prepare the *topping:* Melt the butter in a small, heavy-bottomed saucepan over low heat. Add the corn syrup, white sugar, and brown sugar and bring to a boil, stirring constantly. Allow the mixture to boil for 2 minutes exactly, without stirring. Remove from the heat and stir in the cream. Pour the mixture into the greased mold. Sprinkle the chopped peanuts evenly over the syrup. Set aside.

To prepare the *batter:* Sift the cake flour, baking powder, and salt together onto a piece of wax paper or into a bowl and set aside. With an electric mixer, beat the butter and brown sugar in a medium bowl until combined. Add the egg and vanilla extract and beat until blended and smooth. In a small bowl combine the buttermilk, molasses, and baking soda. The mixture will foam. Add it to the butter-sugar-egg mixture alternately with the sifted dry ingredients, beginning and ending with the dry ingredients. Beat at low

The New Yorker Café teapot: Henry Cavanagh Kingston, N.Y. 1993

◆ *(top) Brownstone Peanut Cake (page 97)*

◆ *(bottom) Mrs. Casey's Raisin Brownstone Cake (page 100)*

speed until thoroughly combined and smooth. Pour and scrape the batter evenly over the peanuts in the prepared pan. Smooth the top with a rubber spatula. Bake in the middle of the oven for 35 to 40 minutes until a wooden toothpick inserted in the center comes out clean, with no uncooked batter on it. Wait 1 minute before turning the cake out onto a wire rack. If some peanuts remain in the pan, scrape them out and put them on the cake. Allow the cake to cool thoroughly. After several hours the syrup will seep into the top of the cake, leaving the peanuts caramelized but not sticky. (Delicious!) Use a serrated knife and a sawing motion to cut through the hard topping and soft cake.

Yield: 6 small portions

> The term TIP dates to the eighteenth century. Twining's London tea house displayed coin boxes encouraging offerings from the patrons "To Insure Promptness."

Mrs. Casey's Raisin Brownstone Cake

Mrs. Casey is the mother of a friend of a friend, and I have never met her. However, I admire her tremendously because this recipe really does seem to be foolproof. I have made the cake in an 8-inch tube pan, a 6-cup Bundt pan, a 9-inch-by-3½-inch loaf pan, and a 9-inch-by-5-inch loaf pan and it is always moist and delicious. Generally, I prefer plain, unfrosted cakes at teatime, but this is an exception. The mocha topping is a delightful addition to the cake. Brown inside and out, my version of Mrs. Casey's cake:

2 cups water
1 cup raisins
2 cups all-purpose flour (sift before measuring)
2 tablespoons unsweetened cocoa powder, preferably Dutch-processed
1 teaspoon ground cinnamon
¼ teaspoon ground cloves

pinch of nutmeg, preferably freshly ground
½ cup (1 stick) unsalted butter, softened
1 cup granulated sugar
1 egg, graded large
1 teaspoon pure vanilla extract
½ teaspoon instant-coffee powder
1 teaspoon baking soda

Bring the water and raisins to a boil in a saucepan and simmer gently for 10 minutes. Remove from the heat and let cool for at least 1 hour and at most overnight.

When you are ready to bake, position an oven rack in the center of the oven and preheat the oven to 350 degrees. Grease a cake pan with a 6- to 7-cup capacity with butter or no-stick cooking spray, dust it lightly with flour, and tap out the excess. Set the pan aside.

Measure the flour, cocoa, cinnamon, cloves, and nutmeg into a medium bowl and whisk until the cocoa is evenly distributed. Set aside.

In a large bowl with an electric mixer or by hand with a wooden spoon, cream the butter and sugar until fluffy. Add the egg and the vanilla and beat until incorporated. In a small cup dissolve the coffee powder in 1 tablespoon of the raisin liquid and add it to the batter. With a wooden spoon or spatula, stir in half the dry ingredients. Stir the baking soda into the raisins; the liquid may fizz. Add the raisin mixture, all at once, to the batter and mix. Finally, add the remaining dry ingredients and stir until smooth. The batter will be thin. Pour it into the prepared pan and tap the pan sharply against the countertop to break any bubbles in the batter.

Bake the cake in the center of the oven for about 55 to 60 minutes or until a wooden toothpick inserted in the center of the cake comes out clean, with no uncooked batter on it. The top may have cracked during baking; it is to be expected. Remove the cake from the oven and place the pan on a rack. After 10 minutes, run a sharp knife around the edge of the cake to loosen it from the pan and turn it out onto a wire rack. Allow the cake to remain on the rack until it is completely cool to the touch. Spread with mocha frosting (recipe follows).

Yield: 8 portions

If an iced cake is too messy to pack and transport to a picnic tea, try this: slice the uniced cake and spread one side of the slices with icing; sandwich together and wrap.

Mocha Frosting

◆

2 cups confectioners' sugar, sifted
1 tablespoon unsweetened cocoa powder, preferably Dutch-processed
2 tablespoons unsalted butter, softened

1 teaspoon instant-coffee powder dissolved in 2 tablespoons warm water
¼ teaspoon pure vanilla extract
1 teaspoon milk (or more, as needed)

Stir the sugar and cocoa powder together in a medium bowl. Add the softened butter and combine. Add the coffee and vanilla extract and beat until the mixture is thick but spreadable. If it is too thick, add milk, a few drops at a time, until it reaches the desired consistency. Frost the top of the raisin cake.

Bake layer cakes and square cakes in the *center* of the oven, loaf cakes or tube cakes in the *lower third* of the oven.

Tailgate Crumb Cake

Sour cream cakes with a crumb topping, baked and served from the same pan, are usually called coffee cakes. This particular one is delicious with tea or coffee or just about any beverage, hot or cold. It is well suited for picnic teas because it travels easily. When the pan is completely cool to the touch, simply cover it with a double thickness of aluminum foil, crimp the edges, and place it in your picnic basket.

Filling:
¼ cup granulated sugar
¼ cup pecans, chopped to pea size
½ teaspoon cinnamon

Topping:
½ cup unsifted all-purpose flour
½ cup granulated sugar
½ teaspoon cinnamon
¼ cup (½ stick) cold unsalted butter, cut into bits

Batter:
2 cups unsifted cake flour
1 teaspoon baking powder
1 teaspoon baking soda
pinch of salt
½ cup (1 stick) unsalted butter, softened
¾ cup granulated sugar
2 eggs, graded large
1 cup dairy sour cream
1 teaspoon pure vanilla extract

Position an oven rack in the center of the oven and preheat the oven to 350 degrees. Thoroughly grease a 9-inch square pan with butter or no-stick cooking spray and set aside.

To prepare the *filling:* In a small bowl toss together the sugar, pecans, and cinnamon. Set aside.

To prepare the *topping:* In a medium bowl combine the flour, sugar, and cinnamon. Using a pastry blender or 2 table knives, cut in the bits of butter until they are about the size of peas. Set aside.

To prepare the *batter:* Sift the cake flour, baking powder, baking soda, and salt together onto a large piece of wax paper or into a medium bowl and set aside. Using an electric mixer, beat the stick of softened butter with the sugar until fluffy. Beat in the eggs, one at a time, mixing thoroughly. Stir in the sour cream and vanilla extract and beat on low speed until smooth. Add the sifted dry ingredients and combine at low speed. Increase mixer speed to medium and beat for 1 minute. Spoon half the batter into the prepared pan and sprinkle the surface with the pecan filling. Carefully spoon the remaining batter over the filling. Use the back of a spoon or a table knife to smooth the batter, taking care not to disturb the filling. Sprinkle the butter-flour topping evenly over the surface. Bake in the center of the oven for about 50 minutes or until a wooden toothpick inserted deep into the center of the cake comes out clean, with no unbaked batter on it. Place the pan on a rack to cool thoroughly. (The cake is delicious when warm, but if you are planning to pack it, don't cover it while it is still warm, or it will sweat.) When ready to serve, run a sharp knife between the cake and the pan to loosen the cake, then cut it into 9 even squares. The squares should come out of the pan easily with the aid of an angled metal spatula.

Yield: 9 portions

♔ *Automobile (License OKT42) teapot: James Sadler & Sons England 1930s*

◆ *(left) Tailgate Crumb Cake (page 103)*

◆ *(center) Chocolate Surprise Muffins (page 106)*

◆ *(right) Cream Cheese and Jelly Muffins (page 108)*

Chocolate Surprise Muffins

♦

The components of a perfect picnic tea can be as simple as a beautiful location, glorious weather, a thermos of tea, and a basket of filled muffins. No need to pack butter, jam, or other spreads; these muffins emerge from the oven complete and ready to go!

3 ounces (3 squares) unsweetened
chocolate
1 cup granulated sugar, divided
2 cups unsifted all-purpose flour
2 teaspoons unsweetened cocoa powder
1½ teaspoons baking powder
½ teaspoon baking soda
½ cup (1 stick) unsalted butter, softened
2 eggs, graded large

1 teaspoon instant-espresso or -coffee
powder dissolved in 2 teaspoons
hot water
1 cup buttermilk, at room temperature
⅓ cup (approximately) thick preserves:
raspberry, ginger, or pineapple are
recommended
confectioners' sugar for decoration
(optional)

Position an oven rack in the center of the oven and preheat the oven to 375 degrees. (If you are using muffin pans with a very dark finish, preheat the oven to 350 degrees.) Line muffin pans with paper baking cups and set aside.

Chop the chocolate into small pieces and place in the work bowl of a *food processor* with ¼ cup of the granulated sugar. Process until the chocolate is very finely chopped, almost to a powder, and no larger pieces are visible. Add the flour, cocoa powder, baking powder, and baking soda and pulse until all are evenly distributed. Turn out into a bowl or onto a large sheet of wax paper and set aside.

In a large bowl cream the butter and the remaining ¾ cup of sugar until fluffy. Add the eggs, one at a time, and the dissolved coffee and beat to combine. Fold in the flour-chocolate mixture alternately with the buttermilk, beginning and ending with the dry ingredients. The batter should be lumpy; do not overmix.

Using a measuring spoon and a tiny rubber spatula, spoon 2 level tablespoons of the batter into each of the prepared muffin cups. Place a generous teaspoonful of preserves over the batter and cover it with more batter (about 1 heaping tablespoonful).

Bake in the center of the oven for about 25 minutes or until the tops of the muffins look dry and the centers spring back when gently pressed with your fingertip. Cool in the pan for about 5 minutes before turning out onto a wire rack to cool thoroughly. Serve these at room temperature with a bit of confectioners' sugar sifted on top, if using.

Yield: 18 muffins

If you don't have enough batter to fill all the muffin cups in your pan, spoon a tablespoon or two of hot water into the empty cups before baking. It will keep the pan from burning and provide moisture for the muffins.

Cream Cheese and Jelly Muffins

◆

It can be awkward, even impossible, to balance a teacup and spread a muffin with toppings at the same time. Here is the perfect solution: bake the muffins, cream cheese, and jelly all together. The technique works perfectly if you take a little extra time with the preparation, and the end result is delicious.

3 ounces Philadelphia Brand cream cheese★, very cold
2 cups unsifted all-purpose flour
2 teaspoons baking powder
pinch of salt
6 tablespoons (¾ stick) unsalted butter, softened

¾ cup granulated sugar
2 eggs, graded large
½ teaspoon pure vanilla extract
¾ cup plus 2 tablespoons buttermilk, at room temperature
⅓ cup (approximately) jelly or preserves

Position an oven rack to the center of the oven and preheat the oven to 375 degrees. Line muffin pans with paper muffin cups, set aside.

Using a thin, sharp knife, cut a 3-ounce brick of cold cream cheese into 16 pieces. Place the pieces on a flat plate or sheet of wax paper and press them flat with the back of a spoon. The cheese will not melt during baking, so take the time to make very thin disks. Set aside.

In a medium bowl stir and toss together the flour, baking powder, and salt. Set aside.

In a larger bowl cream the butter and sugar until fluffy. Beat in the eggs, one

★ Other brands are not as firm as Philadelphia and, when used in this recipe, result in muffins that are overmoist and soggy.

at a time, and the vanilla extract. Fold in the dry ingredients alternately with the buttermilk, beginning and ending with the dry ingredients. The batter can be a bit lumpy; do not overmix.

Using a measuring spoon and a tiny rubber spatula, spoon about 2 level teaspoons of the batter into each of the prepared muffin cups. Place a rounded teaspoon of jelly in the center of each and cover with a disk of cream cheese. Top with batter (about 1 heaping tablespoonful).

Bake in the center of the oven for about 25 minutes until the tops are lightly colored and the center of the muffins spring back when gently pressed with your fingertip. Cool in the pans for about 5 minutes before turning out onto a rack to cool thoroughly. These are best at room temperature and should not be served while the jelly might still be very hot.

Yield: 16 muffins

The Ritz's Perfect Pound Cake

The best pound cake I ever tasted (although it was called orange cake, as I recall) was served to me at the Ritz Hotel in Madrid many years ago. I haven't been back, but I did work out a recipe that approximates the dense orange-flavored cake I remember. Pound cake is supposedly named for the weight of its ingredients: a pound each of butter, flour, sugar, and eggs. Those proportions don't work as well as the Ritz's.

dry, unflavored bread crumbs for the pan
¾ cup (1½ sticks) unsalted butter,
    softened
4 ounces cream cheese, softened
1¼ cups plus 2 tablespoons granulated
    sugar

grated rind of 1 orange (zest)
3 eggs, graded large
1 teaspoon pure vanilla extract
1½ cups cake flour (sift before
    measuring)
pinch of salt

Position an oven rack in the bottom third of the oven and preheat the oven to 300 degrees. Thoroughly grease a 9-inch-by-5-inch loaf pan or an 8-inch tube pan. Sprinkle dry bread crumbs over all the greased surfaces of the pan, invert, and tap out the excess crumbs. Set aside.

Using an electric mixer, beat the butter, cream cheese, sugar, and orange zest until fluffy. Add the eggs, one at a time, and the vanilla extract and beat on low speed until blended. Stir in the sifted flour mixed with a pinch of salt and beat on low speed until thoroughly combined and smooth. Pour and scrape the batter into the prepared pan. Smooth the top with a rubber spatula and bake in the lower third of the oven for about 1 hour and 15 minutes. The cake is done when it is golden brown all over and springs back sharply when gently depressed with your fingertip. A wooden toothpick inserted deep in the center should come out clean. The top of the cake may crack while it is baking; it is to be expected. As soon as the cake tests done, while it is still in the oven, carefully (wear oven mitts) cover it with a piece of aluminum foil and crimp the edges. This will keep the top from becoming too crusty and cracking further. Place the covered pan on a wire rack to cool for 10 to 15 minutes. Remove the foil and turn the cake out onto a wire rack to cool completely. It may be necessary to tap the bottom of the pan sharply with the handle of a knife or other heavy utensil to loosen the cake. When cool, wrap the cake in plastic wrap and let it stand at room temperature for

*Bellhop teapot:
Martin and Judy
Bibby
Swineside Ceramics
Wensleydale,
England
1985*

◆ *(top) Hotel
Banana Layer
Cake (page 112)*

◆ *(bottom) The
Ritz's Perfect
Pound Cake
(page 109)*

at least 8 hours or overnight before serving. This resting period allows the flavor and texture of the cake to settle.

Yield: 6 portions of 2 thin slices each

Tea loaves and pound cakes are best baked a day or two before serving. Their flavor and texture improve upon standing at least 12 hours. After baking, cool the cake to room temperature, wrap securely in plastic wrap and foil, and store at room temperature overnight or longer in the refrigerator.

Hotel Banana Layer Cake

My mother has a keen memory for recipes. She brought this one home from a vacation in the Caribbean in the 1960s. She remembers the cake in detail, but has long since forgotten the name of the hotel where she persuaded the baker to share her recipe. Bananas to be used in baking must be ripe. That is, they should have skins speckled with brown. In fact, the browner the skins, the sweeter the bananas, so you may want to adjust the amount of sugar you use according to the ripeness of the fruit. If the skins are all yellow and hard to the touch, the fruit will not be flavorful and will not blend into the batter. To speed up the ripening process, keep fruit in a closed brown paper bag.

dry, unflavored bread crumbs for the pan
1½ cups all-purpose flour (sift before
    measuring)
1 teaspoon baking powder
pinch of salt
6 tablespoons (¾ stick) unsalted butter,
    softened
⅔ to 1 cup granulated sugar (depending
    on the ripeness of the bananas
    used)
½ teaspoon pure vanilla extract
2 eggs, graded large
½ teaspoon baking soda
1 cup mashed ripe banana (about 2 large
    bananas) plus 1 whole ripe banana
    for the filling

½ cup walnuts, ground to the size of
    fresh bread crumbs, plus walnut
    halves for decoration (optional)
¼ cup buttermilk, at room temperature

Cream Cheese Icing:
8 ounces cream cheese, at room
    temperature
¼ cup (½ stick) unsalted butter, at room
    temperature
1 cup confectioners' sugar (sift before
    measuring)
½ teaspoon pure vanilla extract
    (optional)

Position an oven rack in the center of the oven and preheat the oven to 350 degrees. Grease 2 8-inch round cake pans with butter or no-stick cooking spray. Line the pans with baking parchment or wax paper cut to fit and grease the paper. Sprinkle the greased surfaces with dry bread crumbs and tap out the excess. Set aside.

Sift the flour, baking powder, and salt together onto a piece of wax paper and set aside.

With an electric mixer, cream the butter and sugar until light and fluffy. Add the vanilla extract and the eggs, one at a time, and beat until thoroughly combined. Stir the baking soda into the mashed banana and add to the batter along with the ground walnuts. Stir to incorporate. Gradually add the flour mixture alternately with the buttermilk, beginning and ending with the flour. Beat briefly at low speed, scraping the sides of the bowl with a rubber spatula as often as necessary. Pour and scrape the batter evenly into the 2 prepared pans and smooth the tops. Bake the cakes in the center of the oven for about 30 minutes until the tops spring back when gently pressed with your fingertip and a wooden toothpick inserted in the centers comes out clean. Turn the cakes out onto wire racks, remove the paper, and invert them onto other wire racks to cool right side up.

To make the icing: Place the cream cheese, butter, and sugar in the bowl of a food processor or electric mixer. The addition of vanilla extract will enhance the taste but muddy the color of the icing. Add it or not. Process or beat briefly until the mixture is smooth.

Place one of the cooled layers on a flat serving plate. Spread icing on the top, leaving a ¼-inch margin all around. Do not ice the sides. Slice 1 banana into even ¼-inch rounds and cover the icing with a single layer of them. Do not place any banana on the margin of uniced cake or it might squirt out from between the layers when the cake is cut. Place the second cake over the sliced bananas and spread icing on top of it. Do not ice the sides. Decorate with walnut halves if you wish. The cake can be refrigerated briefly to firm up the icing before serving. To serve, cut with a sawing motion.

Yield: 8 portions

> When baking 2 pans in the same oven, allow at least 1 inch between the pans and at each side of the oven if they are on the same oven rack. If they are on different racks, don't place one pan directly over the other. The object is to provide as much air circulation as possible. The baking time is likely to be a bit longer than for 1 pan.

Pop's Diner Poppy Seed Cake

◆

Typical diner food (often heavy and greasy) doesn't have much in common with the dainty foods one associates with teatime, but there are exceptions. This lemon-flavored poppy seed cake tastes very much like the one I remember eating at a local diner when I was growing up on Long Island, New York. As I recall, Pop used to make his in a loaf shape and serve thick slabs of it, usually with coffee. I bake it in a miniature Kugelhopf mold, sprinkle it with powdered sugar, and serve thin slices with hot or iced tea. Poppy seeds, whose flavor is somewhat like walnuts, are sold in little jars in the spice section of grocery stores.

1 cup cake flour (sift before measuring)
1 teaspoon baking powder
3 tablespoons poppy seeds
¼ cup (½ stick) unsalted butter, softened
¾ cup granulated sugar, divided

grated rind of 1 lemon (zest)
½ cup milk, at room temperature
2 egg whites, graded large
pinch of salt
confectioners' sugar for decoration

Position an oven rack in the center of the oven and preheat the oven to 350 degrees. You will need a 5- or 6-cup tube pan, preferably one with a design. I use a 6½-inch Kugelhopf mold made in Germany by Kaiser. An 8-inch Bundt pan also makes an attractive small cake. (Note: For a larger cake, simply double the recipe and use a 10- or 12-cup tube pan; the baking time is just about the same.) Thoroughly grease the pan with butter or no-stick cooking spray, taking care to grease all the nooks and crannies, including the tube. Dust the greased surfaces with flour and tap out the excess. Set aside.

In a small bowl combine the cake flour, baking powder, and poppy seeds and stir with a wire whisk or fork until the seeds are evenly distributed. Set aside.

With an electric mixer, cream the butter. Gradually add ½ cup plus 2 teaspoons of granulated sugar and the lemon zest. Beat until light and fluffy. Add the milk, in thirds, alternately with the dry ingredients, in thirds, beginning with the milk and ending with the dry ingredients. Beat only until combined.

In a separate bowl with clean beaters, beat the egg whites until they froth. Add a pinch of salt and continue beating until they begin to hold a shape when the beaters are lifted. Gradually add the remaining 2 tablespoons of granulated sugar, beating until the whites are shiny and stiff. Gently stir about ¼ of the beaten whites into the poppy-seed mixture to lighten it. Gently, but thoroughly, fold in the remainder of the whites (it may be difficult to detect the whites in the white batter). Pour and scrape the batter into the prepared pan and smooth the top with a rubber spatula. Bake for 45 to 50 minutes until the top of the cake is golden brown all over, the top springs back when gently pressed with your fingertip, and a wooden toothpick inserted in the center comes out clean. The cake will puff up above the top of a 5-cup pan during the latter part of the baking time but will sink down again. Allow the cake to rest in the pan on a wire rack for 10 minutes before turning it out onto a wire rack to cool completely. Before serving, sift a bit of confectioners' sugar through a fine strainer over the top of the cake.

Yield: 4 to 5 small portions

Don't try to remove batter from a spoon or spatula by banging it against the bowl; the blows are likely to deflate the air that has been beaten into the batter.

Diner teapot: Jerry Berta Rockford, Michigan 1990

◆ *(left) Pop's Diner Poppy Seed Cake (page 115)*

◆ *(right) Pineapple Cheesecake Bites (page 118)*

Pineapple Cheesecake Bites

At a wonderful, old-fashioned diner in Woodbury, Connecticut, I learned to like cheesecake, or, more accurately, cheese pie. Served in wedges from aluminum pie plates, it is typical diner fare. However, with some slight modifications, this creamy, crunchy, fruity dessert becomes a perfect teatime sweet, suitable for the most elegant tea party. Because these are best after an overnight chilling, you should plan to make them the day before you want to serve them.

Crust:
1 cup graham cracker crumbs (about 8
    double crackers)
¼ cup (½ stick) unsalted butter, melted
pinch of powdered ginger

Cheese Filling:
8 ounces Philadelphia Brand cream
    cheese★
⅓ cup granulated sugar
1 egg, graded large

2 tablespoons heavy cream
½ teaspoon pure vanilla extract
1 teaspoon grated lemon rind (zest)

Topping:
1 8-ounce can crushed pineapple in
    unsweetened juice
2 teaspoons granulated sugar
1½ teaspoons cornstarch
1 teaspoon light rum
1 drop yellow food coloring (optional)

Position 2 oven racks to divide the oven into thirds and preheat the oven to 375 degrees. Thoroughly grease 24 minimuffin cups with butter or no-stick cooking spray and set aside.

In a medium bowl combine the crust ingredients until well blended and divide among the greased muffin cups (about 1 scant tablespoon each). With

★ Philadelphia Brand cream cheese is denser than other brands.

your thumb, press the crust mixture evenly into the bottoms and up the sides of the cups. It takes some time to do this so that the sides are uniform, but the result is worth it. Set the pan (or pans) aside.

To make the filling in a *food processor:* Process the cream cheese and sugar until combined. Scrape the sides of the work bowl with a rubber spatula and add the egg. Pulse until the egg disappears. Scrape the sides of the work bowl. Add the cream, vanilla extract, and lemon zest and pulse briefly until all ingredients are incorporated and the mixture is smooth.

To make the filling with an *electric mixer:* The cream cheese should be at room temperature. Combine it with the sugar and lemon zest in a medium-size bowl and beat at medium speed until completely smooth. Add the egg and beat until it is incorporated. Beat in the cream and the vanilla and beat just until all the ingredients are incorporated and the mixture is smooth.

Spoon the filling, which will be thin, into the muffin cups, filling them almost, but not quite, to the top of the crusts. Depending on the size of your minimuffin cups, there may be filling left over.

If you are using 2 pans, place each on a baking sheet and place on 2 racks in the oven. Rotate the sheets top to bottom and front to back halfway through the baking time to ensure even baking. If you have a single pan with 24 cups, place it on a baking sheet and use the upper oven rack. Bake for 12 minutes or until the filling puffs up and barely shakes when the pan is moved. Place the pans on wire racks and allow to cool thoroughly. When the pan is cool to the touch, refrigerate the cakes for at least 2 hours.

To prepare the *topping:* Pour the pineapple into a sieve set over a bowl and, with the back of a spoon, press out the juice and reserve. Combine the sugar and cornstarch in a small, heavy saucepan and set over medium heat. Gradually add a scant ½ cup of the reserved pineapple juice, stirring constantly until the mixture begins to boil. Reduce the heat and boil for 1 minute. Remove from the heat and stir in the rum and drop of food coloring, if you are using it. Fold in the crushed pineapple. Set aside to cool.

Spoon 1 teaspoon of the thickened pineapple, or more if you like, on top of each little cake. (The tops will have sunk during the cooling period.) Return the pans to the refrigerator for several hours or, preferably, overnight.

To remove the cheesecakes from the pans, fill a large skillet with about an inch or less of hot water and hold the bottom of the pan in the hot water for 30 seconds. Take care not to let the water wash over the top of the pan. Use the point of a small, sharp knife to loosen the cakes gently. They should come out easily. Serve cold.

Yield: 24 bite-size cheesecakes

Graham flour is named for Sylvester Graham (1794-1851), a Presbyterian minister who preached temperance. He believed that a strict vegetarian diet, including wheaten products, would suppress any interest in alcoholic beverages.

Elephant Tusks
(Almond Rusks)

After spending a weekend with us, my five-year-old niece reported to her mother that I had served elephant tusks as an afternoon snack. We're not sure, but we think she meant almond rusks. Though they are known by several other names (*biscotti, mandelbrot, zwieback*), in my family, they will always be elephant tusks. The butter and baking powder in these rusks make them lighter and easier on your jaw than commercial Italian *biscotti,* but they won't keep indefinitely, the way some *biscotti* will. They retain their freshness for only about 2 weeks in an airtight container.

1 cup unblanched almonds
½ cup (1 stick) unsalted butter, softened
1 cup granulated sugar
3 eggs, graded large
½ teaspoon pure vanilla extract
⅛ teaspoon pure almond extract

2 tablespoons crushed anise seeds
  (optional)
1½ teaspoons baking powder
pinch of salt
2¾ cups unsifted all-purpose flour

Preheat the oven or a toaster oven to 350 degrees. Spread the almonds in a single layer in a baking pan and bake for 10 minutes until lightly toasted and fragrant. Remove from the oven and cool. When cool, cut them in half or thirds and set aside.

In a large bowl cream the butter and sugar until fluffy. Beat in the eggs, one at a time, and add the extracts and the anise seeds, if you are using them. Stir the baking powder and salt into the flour and gradually add them to the butter mixture. When they are incorporated, fold in the almonds. Divide the

dough in half, wrap each portion in wax paper or plastic wrap, and refrigerate for at least 2 hours.

When you are ready to bake, position 2 oven racks to divide the oven into thirds. Preheat the oven to 375 degrees. Line a large cookie sheet with baking parchment or aluminum foil, shiny side up.

The chilled dough will be sticky, so flour your hands and work quickly. Shape each portion of dough into a long, flattened log 2 inches wide and 1 inch high, and place them 3 to 4 inches apart on the lined cookie sheet. You will probably have to reshape the logs once you get them on the cookie sheet. Bake the logs on the upper rack of the oven for 25 to 30 minutes until they have spread, are golden brown all over, and feel firm to the touch. Rotate the sheet front to back after 15 minutes to ensure even baking. Remove the cookie sheet from the oven and slide the parchment or foil onto a flat surface. Allow the loaves (they are no longer logs) to cool for 10 minutes before attempting the next step. Reduce the oven temperature to 275 degrees.

Using a pancake turner and your hand, transfer a loaf to a cutting board. Cutting through the warm dough and the nuts without pulling it all apart is a bit tricky, so work slowly and carefully. First use a serrated knife to gently saw partway through the dough every ½ inch. Now use a thin, sharp knife in the same places and press down firmly to cut all the way through the nuts and dough. Carefully transfer each slice with a metal spatula to the cookie sheet. Place them standing up about 1 inch apart on the sheet. (If the slices don't stand up, lay them first on one cut side, close but not touching each other, and then turn them halfway through the baking time. You may need a second cookie sheet.) Bake the slices on the upper rack for 25 to 30 minutes until they feel dry. (If you have used 2 sheets, bake them at the same time, rotating them front to back and top to bottom halfway through the

Elephant teapot: Shawnee Pottery Zanesville, Ohio 1940s

◆ *(top) Jumbo Blueberry Muffins (page 124)*

◆ *(bottom) Elephant Tusks (page 121)*

baking time.) Cool them completely on a wire rack. Store the rusks in an airtight container.

Yield: 4 dozen rusks

> If you are baking 2 identical sheets of cookies in the same oven, but not putting them in at the same time, place a bit of rolled-up aluminum foil in the corner of the baking sheet that goes in first. The sheet with the bit of foil comes out first.

Jumbo Blueberry Muffins

As a rule, I prefer small finger foods at teatime, but here is an exception. I began making extra-big blueberry muffins to accommodate the extra-big frozen blueberries available out of season, and now I make them all year round. Everyone seems to love them, so I usually have several in my freezer. They're the perfect thing to serve when a friend or neighbor drops by. They go right from the freezer to a 350-degree oven for 10 to 15 minutes. You will need a muffin tin with extra-large cups. Mine have a 3½-inch diameter and are 2 inches deep.

Muffins:

¾ cup buttermilk, at room temperature

⅓ cup light or dark brown sugar, firmly
    packed

¼ cup (½ stick) butter, melted and
    cooled

1 egg, graded large

1 teaspoon grated lemon rind (zest)

1¾ cups unsifted all-purpose flour

1 tablespoon baking powder

¼ teaspoon baking soda

pinch of salt

1 cup fresh or frozen blueberries (do not
    thaw)

Crumb Topping:

¼ cup unsifted all-purpose flour

2 tablespoons dark brown sugar, firmly
    packed

pinch of cinnamon

2 tablespoons softened butter

Position an oven rack in the center of the oven and preheat the oven to 400 degrees. Grease the muffin cups with butter or no-stick cooking spray or line the cups with extra-large paper baking cups. Set aside.

Prepare the crumb topping first. (Muffins should be placed in the oven as soon as possible after the liquid and dry ingredients are mixed, so it is best to have everything ready beforehand.) In a small bowl combine all the topping ingredients with a pastry blender or 2 table knives until the mixture looks crumbly and no pieces of butter are larger than a pea. Set aside.

In a medium bowl mix the buttermilk, sugar, butter, egg, and lemon zest until combined. In a large bowl, stir and toss together the flour, baking powder, baking soda, and salt. Stir in the blueberries. Pour the liquid mixture over the flour mixture and gently fold together just until no flour is visible. Do not overmix. Spoon the batter into the prepared muffin cups, filling them halfway. Spoon the crumb topping over the muffins, about 1 rounded tablespoon for each. Bake in the center of the oven for about 25 minutes or until a wooden toothpick inserted in the center of a muffin comes out clean, with no uncooked batter on it. Allow the muffins to rest in the pan

◆◆

for about 10 minutes before carefully turning them out onto a rack to cool completely. They are best at room temperature.

Yield: 6 5-ounce muffins

Do not fill muffin cups more than two thirds full or the muffins will be flat and won't rise evenly. If you want bigger muffins, use bigger cups.

Madeleines

◆

Rich and delicious, these shell-shaped tea cakes are soft and light when they're fresh from the oven. However, they dry out quickly. Some, like Proust, believe they are meant to be dunked into tea, but I prefer them fresh and freeze any left over after one day. You will need a special madeleine pan with 12 shell forms. If you wish to bake more than a dozen at once, double the recipe only if you have 2 pans and 2 ovens, or an oven large enough to accommodate both pans next to each other on the same rack. Otherwise, make a second batch from scratch or the butter in the batter will settle while standing, causing the cakes to be heavier on the bottom. Be sure to butter the mold heavily so that a crisp crust will develop at the edges of the madeleines.

Shell teapot: probably Japan 1950s

◆ *(left) Chocolate Madeleines (page 129)*

◆ *(right) Madeleines*

◆◆

◆◆

¼ cup (½ stick) unsalted butter plus 1½
    tablespoons for the pan
dry, unflavored bread crumbs for the pan
1 egg, graded extra-large
¼ cup plus 1 tablespoon granulated
    sugar

tiny pinch of salt
1 teaspoon Grand Marnier or other
    orange liqueur (optional)
½ cup all-purpose flour (sift before
    measuring)
grated rind of 1 orange (zest)

Position an oven rack in the bottom third of the oven and preheat the oven
to 375 degrees. Heavily butter the shell-shaped forms in the pan with softened (not melted) butter. I use my fingers to do this to be sure to coat all
surfaces completely. Dust with dry bread crumbs and tap out the excess. Set
aside.

Melt the butter and set aside to cool slightly.

Combine the egg, sugar, and salt in the small bowl of an electric mixer and
beat on the highest speed for about 15 minutes until the mixture is pale and
very thick. When the beaters are lifted, the mixture will form a rope that
will gradually disappear. Stir in the liqueur if you are using it. Sift the flour
over the egg mixture and fold it in on the lowest speed of the mixer or with
a rubber spatula. Do not mix more than necessary to incorporate the flour.
Fold in the orange zest. Add the melted butter a tablespoon at a time, folding it in quickly but thoroughly. Working quickly, spoon about 1 level tablespoon of batter into each mold, filling them ⅔ full. Do not smooth the
batter; it will level during baking. Immediately place in the lower third of
the oven and bake for about 12 minutes or until the cakes are brown at the
edges and the centers spring back when gently pressed with your fingertip.
Turn out at once onto a wire rack to cool.

Yield: 12 3-inch tea cakes

◆◆

Chocolate Madeleines

◆

A few minor changes in the madeleine recipe make a dramatically different tea cake. This one is chocolate, airy, and equally delicious. Unlike the madeleines (see page 126), which should jump right out of the pan, these can be somewhat reluctant. If you dust the madeleine mold with flour, some of it will adhere to the cakes and detract from their appearance. If you don't dust, the cakes may stick. You can use lots of butter for the molds, hope for the best, and cover up any imperfections with sifted confectioners' sugar.

¼ cup (½ stick) unsalted butter, softened, plus 2 tablespoons for the pan
½ teaspoon baking powder
pinch of salt
¼ cup plus 1½ teaspoons cake flour (sift before measuring) plus 1 heaping teaspoon for dusting the mold

¼ cup cocoa powder, preferably Dutch-processed, plus 1 heaping teaspoon for dusting the mold
¼ cup plus 1 tablespoon granulated sugar
½ teaspoon pure vanilla extract
1 egg, graded extra-large
confectioners' sugar

Position an oven rack in the bottom third of the oven and preheat the oven to 375 degrees. Grease each shell-shaped form of a madeleine pan with approximately a half-teaspoonful of softened, not melted, butter. Use your finger or a pastry brush to distribute the butter evenly over the form. Combine 1 heaping teaspoon *each* flour and cocoa powder and sprinkle lightly over the greased molds. Invert and tap out the excess. Set aside.

Sift together the cake flour, cocoa powder, baking powder, and salt and set aside.

Using an electric mixer, cream the butter and sugar until light and fluffy. Add the vanilla extract and the egg and beat. The mixture will look curdled; it's to be expected. Add the sifted dry ingredients, folding them into the egg mixture on the lowest speed of the mixer or with a rubber spatula. Do not mix more than necessary to incorporate the flour. Place about 1 level tablespoon of batter into each buttered mold, filling each ⅔ full. Do not smooth the batter; it will level during baking. Bake in the lower third of the oven for 9 to 12 minutes or until the centers of the cakes spring back when gently pressed with your fingertip. Remove from the oven, invert the pan over a wire rack, and tap the pan sharply to release the cakes. Cool to room temperature. Sift confectioners' sugar through a fine sieve over the patterned side of cakes before serving.

Yield: 12 3-inch tea cakes

Do not use melted butter when "softened" butter is called for in a recipe; the two produce very different textures in baked goods. To bring inadvertently melted butter to the consistency of softened butter, pour it into a bowl, place that bowl inside a larger bowl of ice water (an inch or two is enough), and stir the butter until it is no longer liquid. Immediately lift out of the ice water.

Apple Cake

Cakes made with oil rather than butter have a dense, moist texture and, though they require more sugar than butter cakes do, they taste less sweet. Tart, firm apples that won't turn to mush while baking are needed for this recipe; Granny Smiths are best.

dry, unflavored bread crumbs for the pan

3 cups all-purpose flour (sift before measuring)

1 teaspoon ground cinnamon

1 teaspoon baking soda

pinch of salt

1 cup tasteless vegetable or corn oil

1½ cups granulated sugar

½ cup light brown sugar, firmly packed

3 eggs, graded large

¾ cup buttermilk, at room temperature

½ teaspoon pure vanilla extract

¼ teaspoon pure almond extract

1 tablespoon Calvados brandy or applejack (optional)

2 cups Granny Smith apples, peeled, cored, and cut into ¾-inch chunks

1 cup walnuts, chopped to pea size

apple-flavored whipped cream as an accompaniment (recipe follows)

Position an oven rack in the center of the oven and preheat the oven to 350 degrees. Thoroughly grease a 9-inch tube pan with an 11- to 12-cup capac-

ity. Sprinkle dry bread crumbs all over the surface of the pan, including the tube, tap out the excess, and set aside.

Sift the flour, cinnamon, soda, and salt together and set aside. In a large bowl, using an electric mixer, beat the oil and sugars until well mixed. Add the eggs, buttermilk, extracts, and brandy, if you are using it, and beat to combine. On the lowest speed of the mixer, or by hand with a wooden spoon, stir in the dry ingredients until incorporated. Stir in the chopped apples and walnuts. Pour and scrape the batter into the prepared pan and smooth the top. Bake the cake for 70 to 80 minutes or until a wooden toothpick inserted deep into the center comes out clean, with no uncooked batter on it. Let the cake rest in the pan for 15 minutes before turning it out onto a wire rack to cool right side up. Serve with apple-flavored whipped cream (recipe follows).

Yield: 8 to 12 servings

Apple-Flavored Whipped Cream

◆

1 cup heavy cream
2 teaspoons Calvados, applejack, or
 apple liqueur

2 teaspoons superfine or confectioners'
 sugar

Using the chilled beaters of an electric mixer, or a chilled rotary beater, or a chilled wire whisk and a chilled bowl, beat the cream until it begins to thicken. Add the brandy and sugar and continue beating until the cream

Apple teapot:
Japan
1950s

◆ (top) Apple Cake
(page 131)

◆ (bottom) Apple-
Cheddar Muffins
(page 134)

◆◆◆

stands in soft peaks. Be careful not to overbeat, as the cream can quickly turn to butter.

Yield: 2 cups

If pasteurized heavy cream (as opposed to *ultra* pasteurized) is available, by all means use it for whipping; it has a more natural, less chemical taste.

Apple-Cheddar Muffins

◆

If there are any left, these muffins should be served for breakfast or slipped into a lunchbox. Although just right for an afternoon tea break, they're good at any meal. The crunchy apple peel and walnuts provide a perfect balance for the creaminess of the cheese.

1 large Granny Smith apple
¼ cup walnuts
2 ounces (½ cup grated) Cheddar cheese
2 cups all-purpose flour (sift before measuring)
1 teaspoon baking powder

½ teaspoon baking soda
pinch of salt
½ cup (1 stick) unsalted butter, softened
½ cup granulated sugar
2 eggs, graded large

◆◆◆

Position an oven rack in the center of the oven and preheat the oven to 375 degrees. Grease 16 muffin cups with butter or no-stick cooking spray or use paper baking cups in the pans. Set aside.

Core the apple but do not peel it. Chop the apple and walnuts into pea-size pieces, and grate the cheese. Alternatively, chop them all together in a food processor (cut the apple into 1-inch pieces before adding), taking care not to overprocess or puree. Set aside.

Using a fork or wire whisk, stir and toss the flour, baking powder, baking soda, and salt in a medium bowl. Set aside.

In a medium bowl cream the butter and sugar until fluffy. Add the eggs, one at a time, beating to combine. Add the apple, walnuts, and cheese and stir. Add the dry ingredients all at once and fold in gently just until the flour is incorporated. Do not overmix. Spoon the batter into the prepared muffin cups, filling the cups ⅔ full. Bake in the center of the oven for about 25 minutes or until the muffins are lightly browned, firm to the touch, and a wooden toothpick inserted in the center of a muffin comes out clean. Let the muffins rest in the pan for 2 or 3 minutes before turning them out onto a wire rack. They can be served warm or at room temperature.

Yield: 16 medium-size (2½-inch) muffins

> When mixing batter for muffins, use a medium bowl. A large one will encourage overmixing, which results in uneven, tough muffins.

See p. 163.

Treacle Tart

◆

Mr. Pickwick, the quintessential Dickens gentleman, would have actually had treacle (what we call molasses) in his tart, but contemporary British recipes no longer call for it. Today the filling is most often made with golden syrup, a thick, divine syrup somewhere between dark and light corn syrup and much more flavorful, yet not like molasses or maple syrup. It really is unique and, if you can get it, I strongly recommend that you use it; otherwise, corn syrup is a decent substitute. The following recipe has all the elements of a typical treacle tart, plus a few that are not traditional (apple cider, apple brandy, oats), and I couldn't resist adding a bit of treacle.

1 9- or 10-inch fully baked tart shell
(the cookie crust tart shell that
follows, or any other sweet crust)
½ cup fresh apple cider
¼ cup old-fashioned oats (not instant
oatmeal)
1 tablespoon Calvados, applejack, or
other apple brandy
¼ cup (½ stick) unsalted butter, softened

½ cup light or dark brown sugar, firmly
packed
½ teaspoon grated lemon rind (zest)
½ cup golden syrup, available in
specialty-food shops
1 tablespoon light molasses
½ teaspoon pure vanilla extract
3 eggs, graded large, lightly beaten
whipped cream, lightly sweetened

🍵 **Mr. Pickwick teapot: Lingard Pottery England 1930s**

◆ **(top) Hazelnut Shortbread (page 141)**

◆ **(bottom) Treacle Tart in a Cookie Crust Tart Shell**

In a heavy-bottomed saucepan over high heat, boil the cider until it is reduced to ¼ cup. Remove from the heat, add the oats and the apple brandy, and set aside to cool to lukewarm.

Position an oven rack in the bottom third of the oven and preheat the oven to 400 degrees. If the tart shell is frozen, fit it into the pan in which it was baked and set aside. It can be used frozen, cold, or at room temperature.

In a large bowl cream the butter with the brown sugar and lemon zest until fluffy. Stir in the syrup, molasses, and vanilla extract until combined. Stir in the beaten eggs and, finally, the oatmeal-cider mixture. Fill the tart shell *half-full* and place it in the preheated oven. If you fill the tart all the way, it will be difficult—or impossible—to transfer it to the oven without spilling the filling. Once in place, use a ladle or large spoon (and wear an oven mitt) to add filling until it is about ¾ the depth of the shell. The filling will run out during baking if you add it all the way to the top. You may have filling left over. Immediately reduce the oven temperature to 350 degrees.

Bake the tart for 25 to 35 minutes until the filling is golden brown all over and appears set (it won't shake when the pan is tapped). If you insert a knife in the center, it will come out clean if the tart is done and it will leave a mark. If, during baking, the pastry browns too much and is in danger of burning, lay strips of aluminum foil over the edge.

Cool the tart in the pan on a rack for 15 minutes, then remove the rim of the pan if you have used a 2-piece pan. The tart can be served warm or at room temperature. It is traditionally served with whipped cream.

Yield: 6 to 8 portions

According to the venerable newspaper *The New York Times*, afternoon tea is rivaling the power breakfast as the latest setting for wheeling and dealing.

Cookie Crust Tart Shell

½ cup (1 stick) unsalted butter
⅓ cup granulated sugar
2 tablespoons light brown sugar, firmly
    packed
1 egg, graded large

½ teaspoon pure vanilla extract
few drops pure almond extract
½ teaspoon baking powder
pinch of salt
1½ cups unsifted all-purpose flour

Melt the butter in a skillet or heavy-bottomed saucepan over low heat and let it cook slowly until it is fragrant and a rich golden color, about 15 minutes. Stir frequently to keep the butter from burning. Transfer the hot butter to a large bowl and add the sugars. Set the bowl into a larger bowl or basin containing an inch or so of ice water and stir the butter and sugar until thoroughly cooled. It should be the consistency of softened butter. Remove the bowl from the ice water and cream the mixture until it is fluffy. Add the egg and extracts and beat to combine. Stir the baking powder and salt into the flour and add it to the butter mixture. Stir just until the dry ingredients are incorporated. Turn the dough onto a large sheet of wax paper and pat the dough into a disk. Wrap it in the wax paper and refrigerate for at least 30 minutes and at most overnight.

When you are ready to bake, position an oven rack in the center of the oven and preheat the oven to 375 degrees. Set aside a 9-inch tart pan with a removable, fluted rim.

With a rolling pin, roll the dough between 2 large sheets of wax paper to a thickness of ¼ inch. (This is very thin for a fragile tart shell and may be difficult to handle. I prefer it very thin, but it is still good if it's thicker; don't worry.) Lift and replace the top and bottom sheets of paper as often as necessary to smooth any wrinkles that may result from rolling. Transfer the dough to the tart pan by removing the top paper and inverting the dough onto the pan. Gently peel away the remaining wax paper. Press the dough gently in place, including the sides. Trim the edge about ½-inch above the top of the pan and fold in the excess dough to make a ¼-inch thicker border around the shell. Prick the bottom all over with a fork. Chill the shell in the pan in the freezer for at least 20 minutes.

Cut out a 10-inch round of aluminum foil and fit it into the shell. Cover the foil with pie weights, dried beans, or raw rice.

Bake the tart shell in the center of the oven for 20 minutes. Gently remove the pie weights and foil liner and continue baking for 10 minutes or until the pastry is a pale golden brown all over, including the center. Do not underbake. If the edges of the shell become brown before the center is fully baked, crimp strips of aluminum foil all around the edge and continue to bake. Remove the pan from the oven and set it on a wire rack to cool for 15 minutes, then remove the rim of the pan. When the shell is thoroughly cooled, carefully remove it from the bottom disk. If you are not going to fill the shell at once, store it in an extra-large plastic bag. It can be frozen, airtight in a plastic bag, for up to 1 month. Defrost it in the wrapping.

Yield: 1 9-inch tart shell or 5 4½-inch shells

NOTE: Leftover dough makes delicious butter cookies: Roll to ¼-inch thickness, cut into squares, sprinkle with cinnamon-sugar, and bake at 375 degrees until golden brown. Cool on a wire rack.

To keep metal pans from rusting, wash and dry them (according to the manufacturer's instructions) as soon as possible after using and place them in the still-warm (not hot) oven to dry completely.

Hazelnut Shortbread

◆

I love this recipe not only because it produces perfect, rich shortbread but because it reminds me of differences between American and British culinary terms. For years I shied away from recipes that called for ingredients I believed to be unavailable in the United States. While visiting England several years ago, I browsed through a grocery store, picking out all the items I thought I would never see at home. Was I ever surprised to find, for example, that treacle = dark molasses, cornflour = cornstarch, and the various sugars were not so exotic after all (demerara = turbinado; caster = superfine; icing = confectioners'; molasses sugar = dark brown sugar). I waited a long time to try an authentic shortbread recipe, but I'm making up for lost time now. "Biscuits" as British as Dickens:

¼ cup hazelnuts, blanched or
    unblanched
1 cup unsifted all-purpose flour
¼ cup cornstarch
2 tablespoons superfine sugar
2 tablespoons light brown sugar, firmly
    packed

½ cup (1 stick) unsalted butter, frozen or
    very cold
1 tablespoon turbinado sugar (Sugar in
    the Raw)

Position an oven rack in the center of the oven and preheat the oven to 325 degrees. Lightly butter a 9-inch round cake pan or pie tin and set aside.

Place the hazelnuts in the work bowl of a *food processor* and pulse the machine until the nuts are finely ground and uniform, and almost, but not quite, a paste. With the machine off, add the flour, cornstarch, superfine sugar, and brown sugar and pulse 2 or 3 times to mix. Cut the cold butter into 12 to 16 pieces and add them to the bowl. Pulse until the mixture looks like coarse meal, then process until the dough just comes together. Do not overmix. Turn the dough out onto a large sheet of wax paper or into a large bowl and knead a very few times to be sure there are no unmixed lumps of butter or unincorporated flour.

Press the dough into the prepared pan. Although the dough should not be very sticky, you might want to place a sheet of wax paper over it before pressing down to smooth the surface. Pressing down with the bottom of an 8-inch cake pan will produce an even surface. Remove the wax paper. If the dough is higher at the edges, use a fork to press it down off the sides of the pan and make a decorative border at the same time. Prick the dough all over with the fork. Using a knife, score the top of the dough into 8 wedges. Bake the shortbread in the center of the oven for 35 to 40 minutes or until it is lightly browned all over—including the middle—and the center slowly comes back when gently pressed with your finger. Remove from the oven and immediately sprinkle the turbinado sugar evenly over the surface. Place the pan on a wire rack. After 5 minutes, use a sharp knife to cut through the shortbread where it is scored. Allow it to cool completely in the pan on the rack. Store it in an airtight container for up to 1 week.

Yield: 8 large wedges

> There is a British superstition that those who add milk to their tea, rather than pouring it in the cup before the tea, will remain unmarried.

Chocolate-Hazelnut Spokes

———◆———

This is one of my best mistakes ever. Thinking I could substitute commercial nut butter for freshly ground nuts in my shortbread recipe, I was surprised when the result was a very flat, very rich toffeelike layer. I immediately melted chocolate on the top and hoped for the best. What resulted is more candy than cookie and positively delicious. This confection is best served in small portions, so I cut the 9-inch "wheel" into 20 "spokes."

¾ cup unsifted all-purpose flour
¼ cup granulated sugar
¼ cup light brown sugar, firmly packed
¼ cup cornstarch
pinch of salt
½ cup (1 stick) unsalted butter, frozen or
    very cold

¼ cup smooth hazelnut butter, chilled
    (available in health-food or
    specialty-food shops)
¼ teaspoon pure vanilla extract
few drops pure almond extract
4½ ounces bittersweet chocolate (best
    quality available)

Position an oven rack in the center of the oven and preheat the oven to 325 degrees. Line a shallow (less than 2 inches deep) 9-inch round cake pan with a 9-inch round of parchment paper and lightly butter the sides of the pan. Set aside.

Put the flour, sugars, cornstarch, and salt in the work bowl of a *food processor* and pulse just to mix. Cut the cold butter into 12 or more pieces and add to the bowl. Pulse until the mixture looks like coarse meal. Stop the machine and add the chilled hazelnut butter and the extracts. Process until the dough just comes together. Do not overmix.

Turn the dough into the prepared pan and press evenly into the pan with the back of a spoon or, if the dough is very sticky, with a piece of wax paper. Prick the dough all over with a fork.

Bake in the middle of the oven for 40 minutes or until the cake is a dark golden brown all over and bubbling in the middle. Remove from the oven and place the pan on a rack to cool for 2 minutes or so, while you chop or break the chocolate into small pieces. Place the chocolate pieces evenly over the surface of the hot cake, leaving a ¼-inch border around the edge. When the heat of the cake has melted the chocolate (3 or 4 minutes), spread it evenly with the back of a spoon. Allow the cake to cool in the pan on the rack. When completely cool, the chocolate will have lost some of its sheen. Place a sheet of wax paper over the pan, place a cutting board or rack over the wax paper and invert. Bang the bottom of the pan with a heavy knife handle to release the cake. Remove the pan and gently peel off the parchment. Place a cutting board over the cake and invert. Remove the wax paper and, with a sharp knife, cut the cake into very thin wedges. These will keep, covered, in a cool place for several days; however, if refrigerated, the chocolate will become hard and separate from the cake.

Yield: 20 wedges, 4½ inches by 1¼ inches

> Good-quality chocolate is as outstanding in baked goods as it is when eaten plain. It has several noticeable characteristics: a smooth and shiny surface, a tendency to break cleanly, a smooth texture when chewed, and no unpleasant aftertaste.

Wagon Wheel teapot, creamer, and sugar bowl: Frankoma Pottery Sapulpa, Oklahoma 1941–1983

◆ *Chocolate-Hazelnut Spokes (page 143)*

◆ *Pump Cake (page 146)*

Pump Cake
(Apricot Tea Cake)

◆

Here's a little cake (only ¾ inch high) that comes out of the oven already filled and glazed. The glaze is achieved by running water over the cake and sprinkling it with sugar before it is baked—a most unusual technique. The recipe comes from the north of England, where it is believed that it dates from the horse-and-wagon days, when water was drawn from a pump.

1¼ cups unsifted all-purpose flour
1 teaspoon baking powder
pinch of salt
½ cup granulated sugar
⅓ cup (5⅓ tablespoons) unsalted butter,
    cut into bits
½ teaspoon pure vanilla extract

few drops pure almond extract (optional)
1 egg, graded large, lightly beaten
¼ cup apricot jam
1 tablespoon granulated sugar
confectioners' sugar for decoration
    (optional)

Position an oven rack in the middle of the oven and preheat the oven to 375 degrees. Butter a shallow 8-inch round cake pan and set aside.

Stir and toss the flour, baking powder, and salt together in a large bowl. Mix in the sugar. Cut in the butter with 2 knives or a pastry blender until the mixture looks like coarse meal. Add the extracts and the beaten egg and stir until the dough begins to come together but is still crumbly. *To prepare with a food processor up to this point:* Pulse the dry ingredients until mixed, add very cold or frozen butter and pulse, then add the extracts and egg and pulse.

Turn the dough out and, with your hands, form it into 2 even disks. Press 1 disk evenly into the prepared pan. Stir the jam until it is soft and will spread easily. Using the back of a spoon, spread it evenly over the dough in the pan, leaving a ¼-inch margin all around. Place the remaining half of the dough between 2 large sheets of wax paper and, using a rolling pin or the heel of your hand, press it into an 8-inch round. Use the bottom of the pan as a guide. Put the dough, still between the paper, in the freezer for a few minutes to make it easier to handle. Remove the top paper, invert the dough into the pan, and slowly peel off the remaining paper.

Now, if you don't have a pump, slowly run cool water from the tap over the cake. Immediately pour off the excess. Put the tablespoon of sugar in a sieve and sprinkle it evenly over the wet cake. Bake in the center of the oven for about 30 minutes or until the cake is golden brown all over. Let it rest in the pan on a rack for 15 minutes. Run a knife around the edge to loosen the cake, invert it onto a board, and invert it again onto a rack to cool. It can be served warm or at room temperature with a bit of confectioners' sugar sifted over the top, if you like.

Yield: 6 small servings

> Most Indian tea comes from the northeastern area of Assam. Because of its high percentage of caffeine and tannin, Indian tea is a major component of "breakfast blends."

Christmas Cake
(Orange Fruitcake)

Too many fruitcakes are maligned. Many are delicious and deserve to be the main attraction at a Christmas Day or Boxing Day tea. Here I've eliminated the ingredients I don't care for in commercial fruitcakes and doubled those I do like. The result is a rich, walnut, orange-flavored cake with a hint of cognac.

dry, unflavored bread crumbs for the pan
¾ cup (4 ounces) candied orange peel
¾ cup golden raisins
1½ cups walnuts
1½ cups all-purpose flour (sift before measuring)
1 cup (2 sticks) unsalted butter, softened
1 cup granulated sugar

grated rind of 1 orange (zest)
3 eggs, graded large, separated
2 tablespoons Grand Marnier orange liqueur
½ teaspoon baking soda
1 teaspoon warm water
½ teaspoon baking powder
pinch of salt

Position a rack in the lower third of the oven and preheat the oven to 300 degrees. Grease an 8-inch tube pan with butter or no-stick cooking spray. Sprinkle all greased surface, including the tube, with dry bread crumbs and tap out the excess. Set aside.

Cut the orange peel into pieces the size of the raisins and place in a large bowl with the raisins. Cut or break the walnuts into similar-size pieces and add them to the bowl. Sprinkle 2 tablespoonfuls of the sifted flour over the fruit and nuts and toss until it is evenly distributed. Set aside.

With an electric mixer, cream the butter, sugar (added gradually), and orange zest until light and fluffy. Add the egg yolks, one at a time, beating

Ace p. 137

Rudolph the Red-nosed Reindeer teapot, creamer, and sugar bowl: Japan 1950s

◆ **(left) Christmas Cake**

◆ **(right) Cherry Pound Cake (page 151)**

until thoroughly combined. Beat in the Grand Marnier. Dissolve the baking soda in the warm water and stir it in. In a small bowl stir the baking powder into the rest of the flour. Add it to the butter-yolk mixture, stirring on the lowest speed of the mixer.

In a clean bowl with clean beaters, beat the egg whites with a pinch of salt until they are stiff but not dry. Gently but thoroughly fold them into the batter. Fold in the floured fruit and nuts. Spoon the batter into the prepared pan and smooth the top. Bake for 30 minutes, reduce the oven temperature to 275 degrees (without opening the oven door), and continue to bake until the cake is browned all over and a wooden toothpick inserted deep into the center comes out clean, with no uncooked batter on it (about 1 hour and 15 minutes more, *a total of about 1 hour and 45 minutes*). Allow the cake to rest for 5 minutes before turning it out onto a wire rack to cool right side up. When cool, use a serrated knife and a sawing motion to slice. The cake will keep in the refrigerator tightly wrapped in plastic wrap and aluminum foil for 2 weeks.

Yield: 8 portions

> Use pans of a size specified in a recipe or the result may be overflowing, overbaking, underbaking, underrising, etc.

Cherry Pound Cake

◆

This is a wonderful tea cake to serve or give away at Christmas or any other time of year. I first tasted dried cherries in northern Michigan and thought they were sensational, with their strong cherry flavor, tart and sweet at the same time. They make an otherwise plain (but delicious) pound cake very special, and I encourage you to try them. Plan to bake this cake one day before you want to serve it.

1 cup dried cherries, available in
    specialty-food shops
1½ tablespoons kirsch, or other cherry-
    or orange-flavored liqueur
1 tablespoon hot water
dry, unflavored bread crumbs for dusting
    the pan
1 cup unsifted all-purpose flour

1 teaspoon baking powder
¼ teaspoon salt
½ cup (1 stick) unsalted butter, softened
3 ounces cream cheese, softened
½ cup light brown sugar, firmly packed
2 tablespoons granulated sugar
grated rind of 1 orange (zest)
2 eggs, graded large

Several hours or, ideally, the night before baking, place the dried cherries in a jar with a tight-fitting lid. Pour the liqueur and hot water over the cherries and cover. Invert the jar several times so that the liquid is distributed and, ultimately, absorbed evenly. (The alcohol is not noticeable in the cake, but if you prefer you can omit the liqueur and increase the hot water to 2 tablespoons.)

When ready to bake, position an oven rack in the center of the oven and preheat the oven to 350 degrees. Butter a loaf pan with a 5-cup capacity. (Note: If your pan has a black surface, reduce the oven temperature to 325 degrees or the cake is likely to burn.) Dust the buttered pan with bread crumbs, shake out the excess, and set aside.

Sift the flour, baking powder, and salt together onto a sheet of wax paper and set aside. Using an electric mixer, cream the butter and cream cheese. Add the sugars and orange zest and beat until fluffy. Beat in the eggs, one at a time. With the machine set at its lowest speed, stir in the flour mixture until incorporated. Stir in the cherries. Spoon and scrape the batter into the prepared pan and smooth the top. Bake in the center of the oven for 45 to 60 minutes or until a wooden toothpick inserted in the center comes out clean. (Baking times may vary with the shape of the pan used.) The top of the cake will probably crack; it is to be expected. Check the cake after 40 minutes. If it is quite brown on top, cover it loosely with aluminum foil for the remainder of the baking time. Remove the cake from the oven and let it rest in the pan on a rack for 15 minutes. Invert the cake onto a wire rack to cool completely. Wrap it in plastic wrap and set aside overnight before slicing. Pound cakes need to rest for 12 hours or so, while the flavors mingle and the texture settles. Wrapped in plastic wrap the cake will keep for several days at room temperature or refrigerated. It is particularly good sliced ¾ to 1 inch thick and lightly toasted.

Yield: 1 small loaf, approximately 6 portions

If you like a dark crust on baked goods, use pans with a dark, dull surface.

Indian Pudding

◆

Served in firm squares or wedges, somewhat like Italian polenta, this is not, strictly speaking, pudding as we think of it now. Native Americans and Pilgrims may well have dined on a version of this recipe on the first Thanksgiving Day. Over the years suet and maple sugar have been replaced by butter and refined white sugar, but the taste is probably similar to the original. It is equally good served warm, tepid, or chilled; let the circumstances determine how you serve it at teatime.

1 quart milk
1 cup yellow cornmeal, preferably stone-
    ground
⅓ cup (just under ¾ stick) unsalted
    butter
2 eggs, graded large
⅔ cup pure (not blended) maple syrup
½ cup granulated sugar
pinch of salt

½ teaspoon ground cinnamon
¼ teaspoon ground ginger
pinch of allspice
pinch of ground cloves
pinch of nutmeg, preferably freshly grated
crystallized ginger for decoration
    (optional)
whipped cream as an accompaniment
    (optional)

Place a pan of boiling water in the bottom of the oven, position an oven rack in the center of the oven, and preheat the oven to 325 degrees. The steam created will prevent the pudding from drying out during the long baking period. Butter a 6-cup baking dish and set aside.

In a large, heavy saucepan over medium heat, bring the milk to the point where it is very hot and a skin has just formed on the top. Using a wire whisk, stir the milk constantly while adding the cornmeal in a very slow stream. To avoid lumps from forming, beat with the whisk vigorously until

all the cornmeal is absorbed and the mixture begins to thicken. Remove from the heat, cut the butter into 5 or 6 pieces, and whisk it into the cornmeal mixture. Set aside to cool to lukewarm.

In a medium bowl combine the eggs, maple syrup, sugar, salt, and spices and beat lightly to combine. Add this mixture to the cooled cornmeal mixture and stir to incorporate. Pour and scrape it into the prepared baking dish. Bake in the center of the oven for 2 hours. (If necessary, add to the barely simmering water in the pan on the bottom of the oven.) The pudding will puff up slightly and then settle down again and the top will become golden brown. A thin, sharp knife inserted in the center should come out clean. Cool at least 20 minutes before cutting. Garnish with crystallized ginger and/or whipped cream, if you like.

Yield: 10 to 12 servings

> Early-American tea sets often included covered milk jugs, leading tea historians to believe that adding hot milk to tea was a Colonial custom.

> All tea, about 3,000 varieties, comes from a single species of flowering evergreen shrub, *Camellia sinensis*. Herbal infusions do not contain camellia sinensis, and are not, strictly speaking, tea.

Teepee teapot: Clarice Cliff Newport Pottery England 1946

♦ *(top) Amazing Maize Cookies (page 156)*

♦ *(bottom) Indian Pudding (page 153)*

Amazing Maize Cookies

◆

This is an adaptation of an Early American recipe. Native Americans would have contributed the hazelnuts and maize—or cornmeal—and the early settlers would have had small quantities of white flour and sugar. The cookies have a crisp, crunchy texture and are a perfect complement to a cup of hot tea.

1 cup unsifted all-purpose flour
1 cup yellow cornmeal
pinch of salt
1 teaspoon baking powder
¾ cup (1½ sticks) unsalted butter,
*   softened*

1 cup dark brown sugar, firmly packed
1 egg, graded large, slightly beaten
1 teaspoon pure vanilla extract
1 cup hazelnuts (filberts), finely chopped
granulated sugar

Stir the flour, cornmeal, salt, and baking powder together and set aside. Cream the butter and sugar until fluffy. Add the egg and the vanilla and beat until well mixed. Gradually mix in the dry ingredients until just incorporated. Stir in the nuts. Turn the dough onto wax paper, shape it into a ball, flatten the ball slightly, and wrap it in the wax paper. Refrigerate the wrapped dough for at least 1 hour.

When you are ready to bake, position 2 oven racks to divide the oven into thirds and preheat the oven to 375 degrees. Line cookie sheets with baking parchment or aluminum foil, shiny side up.

Pour approximately ¾ cup granulated sugar onto a flat plate or sheet of wax paper. Pinch off pieces of chilled dough and roll them in your palms into 1-inch balls. Gently press each ball into the granulated sugar and place them, sugar side up, 2 inches apart on the lined cookie sheets. With your fingers or the flat bottom of a drinking glass, flatten each ball to a thickness of about ½ inch.

Bake 2 sheets at a time for 11 to 14 minutes or until the cookies are lightly browned all over and slightly darker at the edges. Rotate the sheets front to back and top to bottom after 7 minutes to ensure even baking. Transfer the cookies with a metal spatula to a wire rack to cool completely.

Yield: 6 dozen 2-inch cookies

> Nuts broken into medium-size pieces will measure about the same as whole nuts; finely chopped or ground nuts will measure less.

Dutch Chocolate Tea Bread

Dark, rich, and delicious, this loaf is actually somewhere between a bread and a cake. The flavor and texture improve after several hours' rest, so plan to bake it the day before you want to serve it. For an unusual and wonderful tea sandwich, thinly slice the loaf, spread half the slices with whipped cream cheese, top with the remaining slices, and cut into dainty rectangles or squares.

1¼ cups unsifted all-purpose flour
¾ cup unsweetened cocoa powder,
    preferably Dutch-processed
1 teaspoon baking powder
½ teaspoon baking soda
pinch of salt
½ cup (1 stick) unsalted butter, softened

1 cup plus 2 tablespoons granulated
    sugar
1 teaspoon grated orange rind (zest)
2 eggs, graded large
1 teaspoon pure vanilla extract
1 cup dairy sour cream, at room
    temperature

Position an oven rack in the center of the oven and preheat the oven to 350 degrees. Grease a 9-inch-by-5-inch-by-3-inch loaf pan with soft butter or no-stick cooking spray, dust it lightly with flour, and, inverting the pan, tap out the excess flour. Set the pan aside.

Measure the flour, cocoa, baking powder, baking soda, and salt into a medium bowl and whisk these dry ingredients together until the cocoa is uniformly distributed. Set aside.

In a large bowl using an electric mixer or by hand with a wooden spoon, cream the soft butter, sugar, and orange zest until fluffy. Add the eggs, one at a time, and the vanilla extract, beating until combined after each addition. Using a wooden spoon, stir in half the dry ingredients, then all the sour cream, and, finally, the remaining dry ingredients. Mix only until the flour is incorporated; a few lumps remaining are okay. Overmixing will cause the bread to be uneven in texture. Spoon the batter, which will be fairly stiff, into the prepared pan and smooth the top. Bake in the center of the oven for 60 to 70 minutes until a wooden toothpick inserted in the center of the loaf comes out clean. Cracks will develop on the top of the loaf during baking; this is to be expected. Chocolate burns easily, so watch the cake carefully after 45 minutes in the oven. If the edges seem to be getting too dark, place a piece of aluminum foil loosely over the pan for the final minutes of baking. Remove the cake from the oven and place the pan on a rack. After

Windmill teapot:
Japan
1950s

◆ (left) Dutch
Chocolate Torte
(page 160)

◆ (right) Dutch
Chocolate Tea
Bread with Cream
Cheese (page 157)

10 minutes, loosen the sides of the loaf with a sharp knife and turn the loaf out onto a board or rack. Cover the bottom of the loaf (now facing up) with a wire rack and invert the rack, the loaf, and the board. Remove the board and allow the loaf to remain on the rack until it is completely cool to the touch. When it is, wrap it in plastic wrap and set it aside, at room temperature, overnight before slicing. The bread will keep for about 3 days in the refrigerator. It tastes best brought to room temperature.

Yield: 1 9-inch-by-5-inch loaf

The finial on a teapot lid is called a *knop*. It is a Dutch word and a reminder that Holland was the first European country with a history of tea drinking (from about 1610).

Dutch Chocolate Torte

Tortes are generally made with ground nuts or cake crumbs instead of flour; I use both nuts and crumbs here. The chocolate is Swiss, but the source of the recipe is Holland, hence the name. I like to serve this torte with just a sprinkling of confectioners' sugar because it is rich and moist and doesn't really need any embellishment. However, I must agree with my son, who thinks that it's fabulous with a dollop of vanilla-flavored whipped cream or ice cream, or fresh fruit.

3½ ounces bittersweet chocolate,
 preferably best-quality Swiss
 chocolate
½ cup (1 stick) unsalted butter, softened
½ cup plus 1 tablespoon granulated
 sugar
4 eggs, graded extra-large, 2 of them
 separated
¼ teaspoon pure vanilla extract

⅛ teaspoon pure almond extract
¾ cup (2 ¼ ounces) finely ground
 almonds
¾ cup graham cracker crumbs
 (approximately 12 squares,
 crushed)
pinch of salt
confectioners' sugar

Position an oven rack in the center of the oven and preheat the oven to 325 degrees. Grease an 8-inch round cake pan that is at least 2 inches deep. Line the pan with a round of baking parchment or wax paper cut to fit, grease the paper, and set aside.

In a double boiler over hot, not boiling, water, or in a microwave oven, partially melt the chocolate. Remove from the heat and stir until it is smooth and all the chocolate is melted. Set aside.

In the large bowl of an electric mixer cream the butter and sugar until fluffy. Add the whole eggs, one at a time, then each of the 2 remaining yolks, beating thoroughly after each addition and stopping to scrape the side of the bowl frequently. Beat in the vanilla and almond extracts and the cooled chocolate. Either on the lowest speed of the mixer or by hand with a wooden spoon, stir in the ground almonds and cracker crumbs. In a small, clean bowl with clean beaters, whip the 2 egg whites with the pinch of salt until they are just stiff but not dry. Gently fold them into the chocolate batter until no white is visible. Do not mix more than necessary. Spoon or pour the batter into the prepared pan and place it in the center of the preheated oven.

Bake the torte for about 55 minutes or until a wooden toothpick inserted in the center comes out with fudgy crumbs (not uncooked batter) on it. During baking the top will become dry-looking and may crack. That's okay. Remove the torte from the oven and run a sharp knife between the torte and the pan to loosen it all around. Allow it to cool completely in the pan set on a rack. When it is cool it will have cracked even more on top and shrunken from the sides of the pan. Invert the torte onto a board or plate (you may have to bang the bottom of the pan with a wooden spoon to loosen it) and carefully remove the paper. Gently place a serving plate over the torte and invert it again so that the torte is right side up on the serving plate. Just before serving, spoon confectioners' sugar into a fine sieve and sprinkle it all over the top of the cake, covering the cracks completely. Wrapped in plastic wrap, the cake can be kept at room temperature or refrigerated for 4 or 5 days.

Yield: 8 servings

If your pan has a black surface, reduce the oven temperature specified in a recipe by 25 degrees or the baked goods will likely burn.

---

see p. 149

Ladyfingers

◆

First known as finger biscuits, these dainty cakes were referred to by the poet Keats, circa 1820, as "lady's-fingers." Undoubtedly, the name described the size and shape of these fragile and delicate cakes. As time passed, they were made larger and larger, but they kept their name, more or less. The preparation is a bit tricky but not difficult. Be sure to work quickly so as not

to allow the egg whites to deflate. One of my husband's favorite teatime treats is homemade ladyfingers with chunky ginger preserves sandwiched in between.

⅔ cup all-purpose flour (sift before measuring)
3 eggs, graded large, separated
1 teaspoon pure vanilla extract

pinch of salt
⅓ cup superfine sugar
confectioners' sugar

Position 2 oven racks to divide the oven into thirds and preheat the oven to 325 degrees. Butter 2 cookie sheets, dust them with flour, and set aside. Fit a 15-inch pastry bag with a ½-inch plain, round tip and set aside.

Sift the flour 3 times and set aside.

Using a rotary beater or a wire whisk, beat the egg yolks and vanilla extract until thoroughly combined, about 1 minute.

In a large bowl beat the egg whites with an electric mixer until they are foamy. Add the pinch of salt and beat on high speed until the whites are almost stiff and no longer move around the bowl. Gradually add the superfine sugar, 1 tablespoonful at a time, beating until the whites are stiff but not dry. Pour the yolk mixture over the whites and fold gently with a rubber spatula to barely blend. Sift or sprinkle a third of the flour over the mixture and fold in gently. Add half the remaining flour by sifting and folding, and finally the last bit of flour. Fold only until the flour is just incorporated. Do not overmix.

Spoon the batter into the prepared pastry bag and pipe onto the prepared cookie sheets. Make each finger 3½ to 4 inches long and about ¾ inch wide, placing them about 1 inch apart (they won't spread much). Sift confectioners' sugar lightly over the fingers. Bake 2 sheets at a time for 14 to 18 minutes or until the cakes are barely colored and dry to the touch. Reverse the sheets top to bottom and front to back after 8 minutes to ensure even baking. Remove the sheets from the oven and allow the cakes to cool on the sheets (10 to 15 minutes). Using a metal spatula, transfer the cooled cakes to an airtight container. Lightly dust a bit of confectioners' sugar over the cakes before serving. Store at room temperature or in the freezer.

Yield: 30 ladyfingers

Lady Cake

Dense and delicious, this is a lovely cake for a special tea, and, in spite of the name, not necessarily for ladies only. The contrast of the dark, chocolate glaze and white cake is dramatic and the flavors combine wonderfully. Bake it the day before you plan to serve it.

Batter:
dry, unflavored bread crumbs for the pan
1¾ cups cake flour (sift before
     measuring)
2 teaspoons baking powder
¾ cup (1½ sticks) unsalted butter,
     softened
¾ cup granulated sugar
grated rind of 1 lemon (zest)
½ cup milk, at room temperature
¼ teaspoon pure almond extract
     (optional)
3 egg whites, graded large

pinch of salt
¼ cup (approximately) seedless red
     raspberry jam

Glaze:
2 ounces (2 squares) unsweetened
     chocolate
3 tablespoons unsalted butter
¼ cup heavy cream
1 cup confectioners' sugar (sift before
     measuring)
½ teaspoon pure vanilla extract
pinch of salt

Position an oven rack in the center of the oven and preheat the oven to 350 degrees. Thoroughly grease an 8- or 9-inch tube pan (including the tube) with butter or no-stick cooking spray. Line the bottom of the pan with baking parchment or wax paper cut to fit. Grease the paper and sprinkle all the greased surfaces with dry bread crumbs. Tap out the excess and set aside.

Sift the flour and baking powder together onto a piece of wax paper and set aside.

With an electric mixer, cream the butter, sugar, and lemon zest until fluffy and light. Gradually add the flour mixture, alternating with the milk, beginning and ending with the flour. Scrape the side of the bowl as often as necessary and beat thoroughly after each addition. Stir in the almond extract, if you are using it.

With clean beaters in a clean bowl, beat the egg whites until they are foamy. Add a tiny pinch of salt and continue beating until they are stiff but not dry. With a rubber spatula, gently but thoroughly fold the beaten egg whites into the batter. Because the batter and egg whites are the same color, it might be difficult to see when all the whites are incorporated. To be sure, give the mixture 10 extra gentle folds. Spoon and scrape the batter into the prepared pan. Level the batter by sharply rotating the pan back and forth a few times. Bake in the center of the oven for about 45 minutes (a bit longer if you have used an 8-inch pan) until the top is golden brown all over, the cake has begun to shrink from the sides of the pan, and—most important— a wooden toothpick inserted deep into the center comes out clean. Cool the pan on a wire rack for 10 minutes; the cake will shrink considerably during this time. Run a thin, sharp knife between the cake and the pan (the tube, too) and turn out onto a wire rack. Gently remove the pan and the paper and allow the cake to cool thoroughly. Wrap the cooled cake in plastic wrap and leave it at room temperature for at least 6 hours and at most overnight.

To make the *glaze:* chop the chocolate into medium chunks and place them in a small, heavy-bottomed saucepan with the butter and cream. Place over low heat and cook, stirring constantly, until the chocolate pieces are almost, but not quite, melted. Remove the pan from the heat and continue to stir until the mixture is blended; it probably won't look completely smooth at this point. Add the sugar, vanilla extract, and salt and stir to combine until smooth. Allow the mixture to thicken for 5 to 10 minutes, stirring occasionally.

While the glaze is resting and thickening, unwrap the cake and place it on a flat serving plate. Cut strips of wax paper and tuck the edges under the cake so that the plate is protected from the glaze, which will drip down the sides of the cake.

Put the raspberry jam in a small bowl and stir it to make it spreadable and smooth. Spread the top of the cake with a thin, even coating of the jam. Now slowly pour the slightly thickened, but still warm, glaze over the jam all around the top of the cake, allowing it to run down the sides and middle. When the glaze is set, in 30 minutes to 1 hour, remove the wax-paper strips.

Yield: 6 to 8 portions

Tea leaves are almost always harvested by women because their fingers are thought to be more nimble than men's.

Tea rooms and tea shops began to appear in England in the late 1880s and provided the first respectable establishments where women could dine alone or in the company of other women. Later, in the 1920s and 1930s, tea again played a part in changing social behavior of Britons when young people met unchaperoned to tango and quickstep at tea dances held every afternoon in fashionable hotels.

Wartime Cake

Also called Depression cake, or eggless–butterless–milkless cake, this is a recipe that demonstrates the adage "Necessity is the mother of invention." During hard times, when many ingredients were unavailable, a wonderfully creative baker used what he/she had in the kitchen and came up with this dark, moist, delicious cake. In spite of its many unfortunate names, it is good enough for a tea party in the best of times.

1 cup strong tea or coffee or water or beer

1 cup raisins

1 cup sugar, dark brown or light brown or granulated

¼ cup vegetable shortening or margarine or lard or tasteless salad oil

1 teaspoon ground cinnamon

pinch of salt

pinch each ground cloves, allspice, and nutmeg

1 teaspoon baking soda

½ teaspoon baking powder

2 cups all-purpose flour (sift before measuring)

1 teaspoon grated lemon rind (zest) (optional)

½ cup chopped walnuts (optional)

Place the tea (or other liquid), raisins, sugar, shortening, cinnamon, salt, cloves, allspice, and nutmeg in a heavy-bottomed saucepan and bring to a boil over moderate heat. Simmer for 3 minutes, remove from the heat, and pour the mixture into a large bowl. Cool to lukewarm.

Position an oven rack in the center of the oven and preheat the oven to 350 degrees. Grease an 8-inch square baking pan and set aside.

Stir the baking soda into the cooled raisin mixture. It will bubble up. Stir the baking powder into the flour and add them to the raisin mixture. Mix until the dry ingredients are no longer visible. Stir in the lemon zest and walnuts, if you are using them. Scrape the batter into the prepared pan, smooth the top, and bake in the center of the oven for 35 to 45 minutes until the center springs back when gently pressed with your fingertip and a wooden toothpick inserted in the center comes out clean, with no un-cooked batter on it. Cool in the pan for 10 minutes before turning out onto a rack. The cake is good warm or at room temperature. Wrapped in plastic wrap it will keep well for several days.

Yield: 8 small portions

If you like your tea strong, use more tea rather than a longer brewing time.

War Biscuits
(Coconut Oatmeal Cookies)

It is easy to understand why these cookies were popular among the British, who sent treats to soldiers fighting abroad. They are simple to prepare, taste great, and are remarkably crumble-resistant. Two of the ingredients are typically British and may not be readily found in your local market. However, if you can find golden syrup and desiccated coconut, I urge you to do so. The syrup has a unique flavor and the coconut is unsweetened and dry. If not, use dark corn syrup and flaked coconut. The result won't be quite the same but will be good enough.

1 cup unsifted all-purpose flour
1 cup quick-cooking oats (not instant
    oats)
½ teaspoon baking powder
½ teaspoon baking soda
1 cup desiccated coconut or flaked
    coconut

½ cup (1 stick) unsalted butter
¾ cup light brown sugar, firmly packed
    (use 2 tablespoons less sugar if
    using sweetened coconut)
2½ tablespoons golden syrup or dark
    corn syrup

Position 2 oven racks to divide the oven into thirds and preheat the oven to 350 degrees. Line cookie sheets with baking parchment or aluminum foil, shiny side up. Set aside.

In a large bowl stir and toss together the flour, oats, baking powder, baking soda, and coconut. Set aside.

In a heavy-bottomed, medium saucepan, place the butter, sugar, and syrup. Heat over moderate heat, stirring, just until the butter is melted. Pour the warm mixture over the flour-oat mixture and stir with a wooden spoon until combined.

Using a measuring spoon and a tiny rubber spatula, measure level table-spoons of dough and drop them 2 inches apart onto the prepared cookie sheets. With your fingers, shape the cookies into neat rounds about ⅓ inch high. Make them as uniform as possible; they won't change shape during baking.

Bake 2 sheets at a time for 9 to 12 minutes or until the cookies are golden brown all over and slightly darker at the edges. Rotate the sheets top to bottom and front to back after 6 minutes to ensure even baking. Allow the cookies to rest on the parchment or foil for 2 or 3 minutes before transferring them with a metal spatula to a rack to cool completely. If you have used desiccated coconut, the cookies will be very crisp when cool. If you have used flaked coconut, they will be crisp but chewy. Store the cookies airtight for up to 1 week.

Yield: approximately 40 2½-inch cookies

Less syrup will stick to a measuring cup if the cup is rinsed with hot water before pouring in the syrup. Pour out the hot water, but don't dry the cup.

RESOURCES

Where to find out more about teapots:

Books
◆

China Teapots, Pauline Agius, Lutterworth Press, Guildford, Surrey, U.K.

Novelty Teapots, Edward Bramah, Quiller Press, London, U.K.

The Eccentric Teapot, Garth Clark, Abbeville Press, New York

Catalog
◆

The Collector's Teapot
P.O. Box 1193
Kingston, NY 12401
800-724-3306

Dealers
◆

Judy Posner
R.D.#1, Box 273
Effort, PA 18330
717-629-6583

Carol Silagyi
C. S. Antiques & Jewelry
P.O. Box 151
Wyckoff, NJ 07481
201-934-6528

Barbara Strand and Dan Toepfer
Dullsville, Inc.
143 East 13th Street
New York, NY 10003
212-505-2505

Ruth Weeks
Borrowed Time
672 Uniontown Road
Phillipsburg, NJ 08865
908-859-0097

Department Stores

◆

The Vintage Tea Shop
Bergdorf Goodman
New York City

Antiques for Entertaining™
Neiman Marcus
Beverly Hills, Atlanta,
Michigan Avenue, Chicago

Galleries

◆

Ferrin Gallery
179 Main Street
Northampton, MA 01060
413-586-4509

Mark Milliken Gallery
1200 Madison Avenue
New York, NY 10128
212-534-8802

Newsletters

◆

Exclusively Shawnee
P.O. Box 713
New Smyrna Beach, FL 32170

Our McCoy Matters
P.O. Box 14255
Parkville, MO 64152

Tea Talk
419 N. Larchmont Blvd., #225
Los Angeles, CA 90004
310-659-9650

INDEX

afternoon tea, 16, 38
almond(s)
  rusks, 121, 123–24
  in steamed pudding, 57–58
  in torte, 161–62
apple(s)/apple flavor
  in cake, 131, 133
  in whipped cream, 133–34
  in muffins, 87, 89, 134–35
  in tarts, 136, 138
apricot
  prune bars, 73–74
  tea cake, 146–47

bacon and avocado sandwiches, 32–33
baking cups, 36
baking parchment, 3
baking powder, 5
baking soda, 5
bananas, 87, 89, 112–14
bars, prune-apricot, 73–74
basil
  butter, 63
  and tomato sandwiches, 62–63
  in summer pudding, 61
  in onion tarts, 15–16
batter
  for bread, 158
  muffin, 135
  removing from spoons, 117
biscotti. *See* elephant tusks
biscuits. *See* cookies
black currant tea, 68
blueberry muffins, 124–26
bowls
  for beating egg whites, 7
  mixing batter in, 135
bran banana muffins, 87, 89

bread
  crumbs, 46, 53, 55–56, 57–58, 75,
    77
  drying out of, 33
  in egg and cheese tart, 39, 41
  slicing, 63
  See also sandwiches; tea bread
breakfast teas, 38, 147
brown sugar, 5
brownstone peanut cake, 97–98, 100
brownstone raisin cake, 100–102
bunny bites, 77–79
butter, 6, 9, 130
  basil, 63
  cakes made with, 131
buttermilk
  in cakes, 98, 100, 112–14, 131, 133
  in muffins, 106–7, 108–9, 125–26
  in scones, 25–27
  in tea cakes, 67–68

cake pans. *See* pans
cakes
  apple, 131, 133
  baking, 103, 114
  banana layer, 112–14
  browning of, 9
  brownstone peanut, 97–98, 100
  brownstone raisin, 100–102
  Christmas, 148, 150
  coffee, 103, 105
  cracking of, 111, 162
  crumb, 103, 105
  Dutch chocolate torte, 160–62
  fallen, 9
  frostings for, 101, 102–3, 113, 114
  groom's, 50–52
  iced, 102

in cookies, 27–29
in fruitcakes, 148, 150
in pineapple cheesecake bites, 118–20
in pound cake, 151–52
quality of, 131
in steamed pudding, 53, 55–56
in tarts, 136, 138
in tea cakes, 128
in Welsh rabbit rounds, 75, 77
in whipped cream, 133–34
loaf cakes, baking, 103

madeleines, 126, 128
    chocolate, 129–30
maize cookies, 156–57
margarine, 6
measuring cups, 4
mercury oven thermometers, 4, 9
milk, in tea, 10, 142, 155
mocha frosting, 101, 102–3
molasses, 5, 141
    in cakes, 98, 100
    in gingerbread, 69–70
    in tarts, 136, 138
    in tea cakes, 67–68
molded spice cookies, 95–97
muffin cups, 36, 107, 118–20, 126
muffins
    apple-cheddar, 134–35
    banana bran, 87, 89
    blueberry, 124–26
    carriers for, 79
    carrot, 77–79
    chocolate surprise, 106–7
    corn, 35–36
    cream cheese and jelly, 68, 108–9
    frozen, 79
    jumbo blueberry, 124–26

miniature, 77–79
pans for, 107
reheating, 79
techniques for making, 9, 36, 107, 135

nuts, 3, 8, 51–52, 157. *See also* almond(s);
    hazelnuts; peanuts; pecans; walnuts

oatmeal, 8
    in cookies, 27–29, 73–74, 171–72
oats
    in cookies, 27–29, 73–74, 171–72
    roasting, 29
    in tarts, 136, 138
oil, cakes made with, 131
onions
    in muffins, 35–36
    in tarts, 15–16
    See also scallions
orange fruitcake, 148, 150
orange zest
    in cake, 51–52
    in fruitcakes, 148, 150
    in pound cake, 111–12, 151–52
    in scones, 25–27
    in tea bread, 157–58, 160
    in tea cakes, 128
ovens
    drying pans in, 140
    location of pans in, 114
    opening of, 9
    preheating, 9
    temperature of, 4, 9, 151–52, 162

palmiers. See pig's ears
pans
    color of, 151–52, 162
    dusting of, 9

Credits

◆

Page 34: "Vigne" fabric #2112/03, distributed by Osborne & Little.

Page 40: children's wooden blocks from Zona, New York, N.Y.

Page 54: "Stra" fabric #F201/02 from The Designers Guild Collection distributed by Osborne & Little.

Page 60: tomato place mat from The Pottery Barn, New York, N.Y.

Page 104: vintage Florida tablecloth from The Old Carriage Shop Antique & Art Center, Bantam, Conn.

Page 116: Pop's Diner plate by Henry Cavanagh Diner-Ware, Kingston, N.Y.

Page 122: "Coco" fabric #F830/02 from the Charades Collection distributed by Osborne & Little.

Pages x and 154: vintage stenciled tablecloth from Paula Rubenstein Antiques, NYC, vintage bark canoe from c.i.t.e. design corp., New York, N.Y.

About the Author

◆

STEFFI BERNE lives in New York City. She has worked in museum administration, special education, and fund-raising. Her favorite pastimes are baking and flea-marketing. *The Cookie Jar Cookbook* was her first collectibles-and-edibles book; she is working on a third.